This book summarized in a single paragraph:

"Everyone is aware of two things, namely himself, the seer, and the world which he sees; and he assumes that they are both real. But that alone is real which has a continuous existence. Judged by this test, the two, the seer and the spectacle, are both unreal: these two appear intermittently. They are apparent in the waking and dream state alone. In the state of deep sleep, they cease to appear. That is, they appear when the mind is active, and disappear as soon as the mind ceases to function. Therefore, the two are but thoughts of the mind. There must be something from which the mind arises, and into which it subsides. That something must have a continuous, uninterrupted existence. That is, it must be the reality!"

– Ramana Maharshi

Karina Library Press
2016

Ramana Maharshi: Teachings of Self-realization
Robert Wolfe
ISBN-13: 978-1-937902-29-2 (trade)

Cover painting of Ramana Maharshi by Carlos Grasso.
studio@carlosgrasso.com

Karina Library Press
Michael Lommel, publisher
PO Box 35, Ojai, California 93024
www.karinalibrary.com

Also by Robert Wolfe

Living Nonduality

Abiding in Nondual Awareness

Awakening to Infinite Presence

*The Enlightenment Teachings of Jesus:
The Gospel of Thomas*

Science of the Sages

Always—Only—One

One Essence

Elementary Cloudwatching

www.livingnonduality.org

With thanks

to my muse,

Celeste Gabriele

Contents

Just as a person blindfolded,

and left by robbers

in a jungle,

enquires about the way home

and returns there, so also

one blinded by confusion

enquires of those not blinded

and seeks the Source,

and returns to it.

– Ramana Maharshi

Preface

The legendary spiritual teacher whom everyone recognizes when you say the word "Buddha" has had a meaningful impact on human consciousness for many centuries. Yet, in our own era, another spiritual giant has promulgated teachings equally as profound.

While in the former case, due to the blurring of time, there may be some doubt as to what was said for certain by the Buddha, in the case of Ramana Maharshi the record is no more than a couple of generations distant. Some of the disciples whom he guided to Absolute awareness are alive today; and we can even view them in film clips with Ramana.

Coming from his own experience, his pronouncements were remarkably direct and uncomplicated—and, consequently, effective.

What follows is a compilation of extracts from monographs I've written in recent years which address both Ramana's teachings and the spiritual topics he was concerned with.

This book's primary purpose is to provide a solid grounding in the precepts of nondual awareness—and their implications—through the remarkable teachings of Ramana Maharshi.

Introduction

A Tamil poet, Muruganar, first met Ramana Maharshi when, in his early thirties, he came to Ramana's ashram in 1923. He recognized in Ramana "the embodiment of true jnana [enlightenment]." Parting from his wife, Muruganar was a fixture in the ashram for 47 years, until his death in 1973.

According to phrases from his writings, through Ramana he had "the experience of the undivided reality".

> "I have ended the confusion...and I entered the new life, in the boundless realm...beyond duality...beyond birth and death... thinking, yet beyond the realm of thought...my true nature stands revealed...ever present...the indivisible Self...the foundation of all things...the truth of the Upanishads...the import of all the Vedas...the Absolute."

Ramana once acknowledged Muruganar as "one among the very foremost of devotees."

Muruganar often recorded Ramana's spoken teachings, and rendered these quotations into two-line couplets, though they were not organized into any systematic presentation.

While Ramana was still alive, some 800 such verses were published (as *Guru Vachaka Kovai*). These were carefully reviewed, revised and edited by Ramana, for its first printing.

Although Ramana died in 1950, Muruganar had sufficient material to compose more than 2,200 additional similar verses.

For at least the past three decades, David Godman has been a prolific propagator of the teachings of Ramana, and of Papaji (H.W.L. Poonja). (See book titles at www.davidgodman.org.)

Godman, and two associates, published (in India) in 2004 the first English translation—nearly a two year project—of the above-mentioned verses, titled *Padamalai: Teachings of Sri Ramana Maharshi.*

Considering it "a major statement" of these teachings, Godman also wrote informed commentary. Of more than 3,000 relevant, but repetitious verses, he selected and arranged about 1,750 topically. For clarification in some cases, he also added quotes of Ramana from other published sources, bringing the number to approximately 2,000.

This unique volume, nearing 400 pages, is so thoroughly indexed—nearly 10 pages—that it is virtually possible to (re) create one's own dialogue with Ramana, by topic.

What follows are thirteen "questions" that, in the quest of Self-realization, an enquirer might ask of Ramana. Focusing on his most direct replies, which are summarized with his pithiest expressions, the responses below were abridged in some case for continuity. Tamil and Sanskrit words were replaced with English equivalents. (There is a four-page glossary in *Padamalai.*)

There's no substitute for reading the original volume, along with David Godman's commentary, as what follows is a simplified composite intended to give a general sense of the precepts of nonduality (*advaita*), from the words of Ramana which Muruganar and others brought to public attention.

While the statements in the "answers" are from Ramana (though not necessarily in their original order), the parenthetical clarifications are mine.

As a foreword to the "dialogue" with Ramana (who was called—and sometimes called himself—Bhagavan), this account by a college-professor devotee, G.V. Subbaramayya, is of value.

Bhagavan's manner of speaking was itself unique. His normal state was silence. He spoke so little, casual visitors who only saw him for a short while wondered whether he ever spoke. To put questions to him, and to elicit his replies, was an art in itself that required an unusual exercise in self-control. A sincere doubt, an earnest question submitted to him, never went without an answer, though sometimes his silence itself was the best answer to particular questions. A questioner needed to be able to wait patiently. To have the maximum chance of receiving a good answer, you had to put your question simply and briefly. Then you had to remain quiet and attentive.

Bhagavan would take his time, and then begin slowly and haltingly to speak. As his speech continued, it would gather momentum. It would be like a drizzle, gradually strengthening into a shower. Sometimes it might go on for hours together, holding the audience spellbound.

But throughout the talk, you had to keep completely still and not butt in with counter remarks. Any interruption from you would break the thread of his discourse and he would at once resume silence. He would never enter into a discussion, nor would he argue with anyone. The fact was, what he spoke was not a view, or an opinion, but the direct emanation of light from within, that manifested as words in order to dispel the darkness of ignorance. The whole purpose of his reply was to make you turn inward, to make you see the light of truth within yourself.

A "Dialogue" with Ramana

Q. It is said that there is enlightenment and there is "ignorance." You are said to know about enlightenment. How is one to go from ignorance to enlightenment?

R. We have to contend with our age-long conditionings. They will all go. We have simply to throw out all the age-long concepts, which are in us. Knowledge of "multiplicity" is ignorance. We have regarded as real what is unreal. We have to give up this attitude. That's all that is required for us to attain true knowledge [enlightenment]. "Differences" are a consequence of delusion. All knowledge based on differentiation is only ignorance. Perceiving objects as apart from oneself, the ignorant one is deluded. An ignorant person thinks that an individual "I" exists. To whom does illusion come? To the mind, or ego, who feels *it* is a separate entity: who thinks, "I do this"; or "this is mine." One suffers because of the idea that the *body* is "I". Misery is all due to this deluding connection. It is one's ignorant outlook that one should give up. It causes you needless grief.

Q. By "multiplicity" you mean there's "me," "others," the "world," and so on? But there does appear to be these things...

R. The universe's objects and bodies are illusory appearances. Appearance implies *dis*appearance also: whatever appears must also disappear. In light of the Supreme, all objects disappear. The forms It assumes are only appearances. When It becomes known to be all-pervasive, the [separate]"world" is totally absent. Those who are in the knowing state cannot find anything which is different from themselves. But to those who do not reach this state, everything appears to be different from themselves.

One should not think of It as "this" or "that": can there be greater ignorance than to think of the *One* in *manifold* ways? The ordinary person sees the objects in the universe, but not the Supreme *in* these forms; It is the Being assuming these forms—*and* the consciousness seeing them. That is to say, It is the background *underlying* both the subject *and* the object. The Supreme alone is the reality; the world and the rest of it are not.

The realized person knows that what he sees is not separate from the One supreme reality. He is aware of the one Self in all selves, in all things—eternal and immutable *or* impermanent and mutable.

The ego ["I"] is the basis of all differences; the rising of the ego differentiates Self from oneself. Objects are only mental creations: they have no substantive being. The "objective" world is in the *subjective* consciousness. The Self is the only reality, which permeates and also envelopes the world. Since there is no duality, no [divisive] thoughts will arise to disturb your peace. This is "the realization of the Self" [enlightenment]. You realize your own Self first, and then see if the world exists independently of you. *Now* you feel that you are in the world. *Then* you feel that the world is in you.

The world is your thought. Thoughts are your projections: the "I" is first created, and then the world. But there is no

[such] creation in the state of realization. When once you realize your own Self, and that there is nothing other than this Self, you will come to look upon the whole universe as the Self. Its essence is the same as ours, being One and without form [of its own]. It is immanent in every person and every object, throughout the universe. The totality of all things and beings constitute Self. When one clearly knows the truth of oneself, the idea of "knowing objects" departs.

Q. So, all that I see is the Self—and that "all" includes me? What is it that I suppose is a "me," then?

R. Give up the idea that you are the body, of such-and-such a description, with such-and-such a name, etc. Only grief is possible when one thinks of oneself as a body. The "body" is a creation of the ego. On waking from sleep, the ego arises; then thoughts. The real Self is ever-existent; the body is only a thought ["I" am this]—the first of all thoughts, and the root of all mischief. In deep sleep, there is no awareness of [you as] a body, nor of the world. But you *exist* in sleep, nevertheless.

An ignorant person thinks—through the delusion "I am the body"—that an "individual" *I* exists separate from Self. But it is available to us to be free from identifying ourselves with the body—if you realize your true nature. The ignorant thinks "only the body is myself," whereas the enlightened knows that *all* is of the Self.

The body which "dies": were you aware of it in deep sleep? The "body" was *not*, when you slept; but "you existed" even then. So the body which did not exist in sleep, "exists" now in "waking." *You* exist whether the sense of ego ["I"] is there or not. If you realize you are without form, that you are unlimited, what is there to be seen *apart* [a "separate" body]? There is no connection, during sleep, with the body, the senses, and the mind: on waking up, you identify yourself with them. All that you have to do, hereafter, is see that you do not identify your self with them.

The "universe" exists on account of the "I"-thought. If that ends, there is an end of misery also. In the case of the ignorant, the ego identifies itself with some *object*—simultaneously with *its own* rise: it cannot remain, without such association with objects [e.g. body]. If this tendency to identify itself with objects is destroyed, the ego merges into its *Source*. The *false* identification of oneself with the body—or "I am the body" idea—must go, before desired results can follow. It is the attention turned towards the *body* that causes the distinctions between "you" and "I". If one realizes that the reality is One, where then is the scope for saying "you" or "I"? Otherwise, the "individual" must be maintained on one hand, and "God" on the other.

Q. What I am considering to be "me", then—an "individual"—is the Self as one of its appearances. Recognizing that, what becomes of the idea of "me as this separate person"?

R. The "I am this" thought *forms* the individual *and* its "world". The state devoid of the individual feeling of "I" is the Self-realized state. In this state, there is no room for individual being. There is *no* being who is not All else of which he is aware, or not aware. Yet, in sheer ignorance, he thinks that he sees a universe in diverse forms. But when he knows the Self, he is not aware of separateness from the universe: "individuality" and "other entities" vanish [as unreal], although they persist (in his awareness) in all their "forms."

You are now identifying your self with a wrong "I," which is the I-thought [individuality]. This I-thought rises [on waking] and sinks [on sleeping]—whereas the true I exists always. The true I is not apparent while the false I is parading itself. This false I is the obstacle to your realization. Find the *Source* of this false I: then it will disappear. You will then be only what you *are* now: Absolute being. The false I will end only when its Source is known. As a spark proceeds from fire, "individuality" emanates from the Absolute Self.

Demolishing the ego-sense, to its very *roots*, that is realization. It means "death"—with full awareness. If one dies thus, one is "born" again simultaneously, as the continuously-experienced Self. When will suffering cease? Not until individuality is lost.

Q. Clear. Viewing things as separate—from the One—is the obstacle to realization. And that separation will always remain as long as there is the idea of a "separate me" doing the viewing?

R. An "object" always implies the existence of a "subject" [seen/ seer]. There is no moment when the Self, as consciousness, does not exist; nor can the "seer" ever remain apart from consciousness. There must be a seer, for an object to be seen: but since the Self alone exists, it is *both* seer *and* seen. Without the seer, there are no objects seen: *find* the seer.

When the mind sees [discovers] its own Source, and *becomes* That, it is not as a "subject" perceiving an "object". In the realization, there is neither subject nor object; there is no *thing* to see, no *thing* to feel, no *thing* to know. First, one sees the Self as [an] object; then one sees [perceives] the Self as a void; then there is no "seeing." Only enlightenment is final where there is no [subject vs. object] seeing: there will be no "seer" ["I"]; "seeing"; or "object" to see. You must come to recognize the subject *and* object as *one*; if not, you are destroying the perception of oneness, and *creating* duality: realize the undifferentiated being of the Absolute.

There is mischief, or ignorance, as long as there is an object apart from a subject: duality. There can be no [ego] desire if there is no object. The state of no-desire is enlightenment. There is no duality in dreamless sleep—and also no desire. Whereas, there is duality in the ignorant state—and desire is *also* there. *Because* of duality, a desire arises for the "acquisition" of an object. But when the Self is gained, all desires are fulfilled.

The world "comes to an end" by the right awareness of oneself. In deep sleep, "objects" and "world" do not exist for us. Hence, the "reality" of the world is created by the ego, on its emergence from sleep; and that reality can disappear in resuming sleep. The sage does not "see" anything, because the seeing "entity" ["me"] in him has "died." For those in the Self, there is no [separate] seeing—only being. When the sense of separateness is lost—and the object seen, or the subject who sees, is left behind—it is enlightenment.

Q. So, you're saying that both viewer and viewed are essentially the same One Self—and this is what is realized in enlightenment. When the I is recognized, in its essence, to be nothing other than the Self, the "subject" self disappears; all "other-than-I" objects disappear; and the "dualistic" perspective disappears?

R. Of all thoughts that arise in the mind, the thought "I" is the primal one: it is only after the rise of this thought that other thoughts can arise. Even to say "I am not this" [or "I do not exit"] there must be the "I". The I-thought is therefore the [dualistic] root thought. If the root is pulled out, all other [divisive] thoughts are at the same time uprooted. Therefore, question the root-I: "who am I?"—find the Source. Then all "else" will vanish, and the Self will ever remain, alone.

In enlightenment, the only "experience" is that of *non duality*. In that condition, there can be no other principle that remains in opposition to it: there is no *remnant* of *anything* that is *separate*. The Self is all-pervasive; all "else" is absent. The I is only the Self. If one investigates "who am I?," one will discover that there is no such [separate] thing as the I. It will then be clear that what must remain is one's real being. When the mind has reached this state of establishment in the Self, it is abidance—with the ["individual"] I extinguished.

Once the I-thought has completely died, there is not *even* the thought of "I am Self." [There is only Be-ing.] Even in "seeking" the Self (which already you are not apart from), your *seeking* [desire] denotes *separateness* ["I" seek "That"]. *Who* could *experience* it ["finding"]? If there *is* one who experiences, it would have to be said to be the Self itself.

When there is no one to "experience," where is there a question of an I? Only that which Is remains. That is the [ever-present] Self.

Thus, the [unsuccessful] practices to "destroy the ego" [or the "mind"]: neither the ego ["I"] nor the ["individual"] mind really exists, when you *realize* the pure, *undifferentiated* being of the Self, or Absolute. The "mind" is nothing but "thoughts"; and behind every thought, there is the primary thought, which is the I-thought. When the Self is realized, the I-thought disappears; and something else takes hold of you, that is not the I that commenced the quest. It is the real Self, the *source* of I and its ego. So, "rejection of thoughts" is not necessary; there is no need for an effort to reject thoughts. Anyway, all that one has "learned" will eventually have to be forgotten. The perception of the Absolute, the substratum, will not be obtained until the perception of the *relative*—which is a superimposition [on the real Self]—is viewed as unreal. Only the Self is everlastingly *real*.

Q. Nonduality, then, is the perennial truth which spirituality is offering. All the sacred teachings point to this?

R. Just as all rivers discharge into the sea, they all end in the One ocean. Everyone must come back to the Absolute in the end, because that is the Truth. But *creeds* are mental; they exist in the mind—while the truth is beyond "mind." Therefore, Truth is not confined to creeds. So long as "mind" survives, "religion" will also exist. But no religion will persist in the silence that results from looking within.

It is the ego that comes up, in the form of saying, "my religion should be embraced by all."

In truth, we are everywhere; we are all that is, and there is nothing else [beyond that]. One who is awakened, having known the truth as it really is, and who abides as That, will not deviate from that truth.

The sage is *himself* the Self [Absolute]. There is no one who has *not* known God: ignorance consists in not being aware of this Truth. Loss of ego means gaining Self-realization: knowing oneself is knowing the Self. Peace is stillness of mind; when the mind knows that, in truth, there is not anything to "reject" or "accept", it will abide in Supreme peace. Thus, such peace is therefore extolled as immortal life. If a person "dies" while alive, by *extinction* of the ego, he will not ever grieve for any body.

Q. Nonduality seems to be a difficult truth for people to grasp. Yet it is so obvious!

R. However much one may explain, the Truth will not be clear till one attains Self-realization oneself—and wonders how he was blind to the self-evident (and only) existence for so long. But we know the present exists. There is something which is eternal and changeless. And *we* exist. Let us find out that which *always* exists. For the ignorant, the standard of reality is the [changing] waking state; whereas for the enlightened, the standard of reality is the Absolute. This is eternal by its nature, and therefore subsists equally during waking, dreaming and sleep. To him who is one with that, he is awake to the eternal Self; to him, the world is no better than a phenomena presented in a dream.

There is only one true state: that called consciousness or awareness or existence. What is *real* will always exist. The sleep, dream and waking states are mere [changing] phenomena, appearing upon the state of simple awareness. One whole consciousness prevails all alone. This real state, itself, knows nothing of "waking," "dream" or "sleep". There is nothing apart [separate] in the Self. If one realizes the Self, one will not find anything different from the Self. There are no "others": the Self is the one and only *reality*. And there is only *one* infinite reality.

The truth of one's own real nature is that it is an *undivided oneness*: That is what "you" *are*. The Self exists as *one*; it is only your thoughts that make you feel that it is not. The Self, or God, is not somewhere else—but is inside each of us. In loving oneself, one can only love the Self. Love itself is the *form* of God.

Whatever I do, or consider doing, is really God's doing. Nothing ultimately belongs to "me." The truly enlightened sees the supreme Being immanent in everything, beyond all names and forms. The sage experiences the infinite continuously: God and sage are identical. To know oneself is to know God. God consciousness is not different from one's true consciousness. Is God real? As real as "you" are. Where does God exist? In you. You are the Self: you "exist" always. Nothing more can be predicated of the Self than its existence. And there is only being, in Self-realization, and nothing beyond being. From the absolute standpoint, the sage cannot accept any other existence than the impersonal Self, one and formless. The world of objects, names and form is only the mind; when the mind dies [into the Self], the "world" dies with it. *Only* the Self then remains. The "personal" God is the last of the unreal forms to go. Only the absolute Being is real. Hence not only the world, not only the "me", but also the individual God are of unreality. *Yours* is eternal life. Let a person consider if he has been *born*, or if the Self ever has any birth. He will discover that the Self always exists; then he will abide in the ever-present inmost Self and be free from the idea of birth *or* the fear of death.

Q. You always give me more than I've asked for! So, God does what is done—including what "I" do: Self/self are the nondual One...is the nondual One...

R. You are interested in seeking the source of consciousness: to all deep-thinking minds, the inquiry into the "I" and its nature has an irresistible attraction. Yes, call it by any name—God, Self, the Absolute, or the seat of consciousness—it is *all* the *same*. The point to be grasped is that it is the very core of one's being; the center, without which there is nothing else. God is in all, and is seen *in* the "seer." Where else could God be seen: not "outside," but known within. The consciousness within, beyond the mental operation, is known as God. It is only after seeing That, *within* one, that one will be able to see That in everything.

One must *first realize* that there is *nothing but* the Self— and that he *is* that Self. Then, only, can he view *everything* as a *form* of the Self. There is no difference between God and the Self [which is the "self"]. A person who desires [something "apart"], identifies with the body. But the sage is free of the thought "I am the body." So long as you think you are an individual, you believe in a [separate] God. If one is separate, the "world" and one's "God" will be also. You must look upon *all* "objects" [e.g., body] as God's form.

Through self-bewilderment, one imagines *oneself* to be the "knower," and thus "sees" a few illusory objects. The sage is without that bewilderment: *All* the actions of the sage are the actions of God. When one realizes the Self, the feeling "*I* am doing" vanishes. The source of everything is one's Self. Mental distress and misery appear only because of ego-centeredness; in truth, there is no [separate] one to *experience* misery at all. He who thinks he is the "doer" is also the "sufferer." If one learns one's real nature, there will be no misery. One has to give up one's ["individual"] mind, in surrender; after that mind is given away, there will be no duality of any kind. He who remains separate from God has thus not surrendered.

Q. *Yes, I understand now that God, or Self, is not something apart from me, or this body. Nor separate from the world and its objects. And it is ultimately the source of actions, mind and thoughts—consciousness. The Self, as consciousness, sees itself in "objects"—such as the body, as I experience it. This is Self-realization...?*

R. *Know* the I [as Self], and the *present* [eternal], and consider if anything is "created" [as a separate reality]. Without the "seer," there are no "objects". Seeing and creating are one and the same process. There is really no *creation*, and no *dissolution*. The sage, established in the Self, recognizes this by his knowledge of reality. Thoughts and names-and-forms come into presence simultaneously. The Self has no need to express knowledge, for it *is* knowledge itself. There is, beyond it, nothing to know or be known.

The immanent Reality alone is. It is infinite. There arises, from it, this finite [extension of] consciousness, taking on a limited form [mind]. When this "individual" consciousness is merged in the supreme One, this is Self-realization. For all things, consciousness is the foundation; *because* consciousness is the foundation for everything that arises [as Self], it is *even* the foundation for itself [as mind/thoughts]. Consciousness is the *source* of the "mind". The mind functions as the *link* between the Self, which is pure consciousness, and the body, which is inert [when absent that link].

For this reason, inquiry [into I-am-this-body idea] will lead to the realization of the pure consciousness of the Self. It is the Source from which thoughts [such as "me"] spring; we see that, when we wake up from sleep. In other words, thoughts have their origin in this stillness. It is *thoughts* that make all the difference between the stillness of sleep and the turmoil upon waking. Go to the root of the thoughts, and you reach this stillness. But you reach that in awareness [with waking consciousness]. The sage is not unconscious; he is fully aware of the Self. But the deluded one thinks, "*I* am the one who is waking up." Reality being yourself, there is nothing (apart) to wake up to.

In realization, there is nothing [real] but consciousness. So, there is really no entity by the name of [my] "mind"; because of the consciousness of thoughts, we assume something from which they start [as independently created]. That we term "mind." But when we probe to find what that is, there is nothing [no reality] like it. And after it has vanished, peace is found to remain eternal [no divisiveness]. Can the [tumultuous] world exist without someone to perceive it? Which is *prior*, the being-consciousness or the rising consciousness? The being-consciousness is always there, eternal. The rising consciousness springs forth, and disappears: it is transient.

The world is the result of your mind. Know this mind. You will realize that it is not different from the Self. Through the state of being-consciousness [Self-realization], the life of bliss can be attained—at all times, and in all conditions; in this very world, and this very body. The attainment of the supreme state is the cessation of worries. In that state, there are no individuals, only the one Being. Hence, there is no ground for even the *thought* of death.

Q. So this life is being lived—rather than "I'm living it." The "I" is the Self; the Self is all that is; there's no individual I. All the drama around "individual me" is a consequence of viewing things as separate from the one all-pervasive reality. What is called bliss is "abiding as the Self"—nondual awareness?

R. Bliss is not a special condition that is attained. One's desire for that is born of a sense of incompleteness. Ask "who is experiencing this sense of insufficiency?" It is the "me". Seek its source, and "you" find bliss. Such things as ecstatic emotions are symptoms of the presence of the mind: without duality [me/bliss], they will not remain; Self-realization is where these cannot find a place. Individuality entirely lost, the presence of special "states" cannot find a place. Any great "experience"—irrespective of how much bliss it may bestow—remains for some time, and then leaves. If it is impermanent, it is not the ultimate realization If it is changing, it is not realization. What happiness can you get from things that are external to your self? When you get it, how long will it last? To "be" as the Self that you really are, this is the only means to know bliss. Bliss is the Self of one's own nature. Reject all *things*, and what remains is the innate Self: this is bliss.

The only freedom you have is to turn your attention inward; if you want to go to fundamentals, find out "who" it is that *has* this freedom. As long as individuality lasts, there is "free will"; if there *is*, direct this free will into the inquiry: to whom does this free will *matter*? And to whom do such questions arise? Find out, and be at peace. Freedom from desire is the essential pre-requisite; find out the root of desires, the source from whence they proceed. Find the root of desire, and that will remove it.

You are always free, and there is no limitation to that freedom. The sage's ego has died, thus he does not pursue activities with the notion that he is the doer; instead, like an actor playing his part in a drama—free from [emotions such as] "love" or "hate." Then, there is no agitation of mind, sense of doership, and personality: when all *that* is stopped, there is quiet, stillness. When the mind becomes still, the power of the Self is experienced—as pervading everywhere. When the mind is at peace, one experiences that.

For the person who has realized, whatever he does is for "others" only; and though he does these things, the results do not affect him. The sage helps the "world" merely by being the Self. The best way to serve the world is through this Self-realized state. The effect of this experience spreads all over, like a radio transmission, and whoever wants can tune into it. The existence of a Self-realized being is the highest good—the greatest help that can be rendered to humanity. Even though the help may be imperceptible, it is still there. A saint helps the whole of humanity, unknown to the latter.

All experiences—*or* the absence of them—contain the nature of the Self. Supreme consciousness is "that which is". The experience that people get through the senses, the Self is That. The *seer* of the mind, what is called the witness, is That; and That is *experienced* as the witness. The peaceful, knowing experience that arises from awareness is That.

Q. *All of the choices and concerns that we encounter are embraced in this realization, it seems. This realization is the basis out of which one is to operate, in all areas of life, isn't that so? This plateau of stillness, or equanimity, is the antidote to suffering?*

R. Consider. Your true nature is found in deep, dreamless sleep. Sleep is temporary death. The mind is dormant in sleep: it does not know anything. There are no thoughts in deep sleep. Time, past *or* future; nothing exists for us during this sleep. There is no awareness of the body [as an object]; the "body" does not exist in sleep. The *world* itself is not seen in the darkness of deep sleep—nor in the full light of Self-realization. As a matter of fact, our true nature knows nothing of [separative distinctions as] "waking", "dreaming" or "sleeping": these states are only relative. All these are only mental concepts. There was not "unhappiness" in your deep sleep, whereas you may say it exists *now*. What has happened, that this difference is experienced? This: there was no I-thought in your sleep, whereas it is conceived now. Do worries trouble you in deep sleep? No.

Supreme knowledge is not so that, acquiring it, one may attain "happiness"; it is one's ignorant outlook that needs to be given up: it is *this* that causes you needless grief. The cause of your misery is in "you" as the ego; all unhappiness, all your trouble, is due to the egoic I. You need not super-impose suffering on your self. You will find the bliss of the Self if you seek it earnestly: uproot fear and anxiety; these are impermanent. Where there is duality, fear arises. Merge your mind in the Self, and fear and anxiety will go away. In your present state, if you remove one kind of fear [e.g., of "others"], another will rise up; there will be no end. The "I" is the root. Suffering is only *thought*: what "comes" and "goes" is suffering. The sage knows *all* is of the Self: pain also is of the Self. When the idea "I am doing" is gone, nothing affects a person. Even if one is a great "sinner," one should completely give up even the thought of being a sinner!

That which is, is peace. All that we need to do is keep quiet: peace is our true nature. If we remove all the rubbish from our *minds*, peace will be manifest: it is *that* which is the *obstruction* to peace. So, stillness is the true aim of the seeker. That which is, is stillness. In silence, one is in intimate contact with the surroundings. Otherwise, the ego/mind raises difficulties, obstacles, and then one suffers from the perplexity of apparent [dualistic] paradoxes. If one examines the ephemeral nature of external phenomena, it results in a disinterest in wealth, fame, ease, pleasure, etc. Therefore, the saints are said to be helpful even though they remain in forests. If you give up all desires, what remains is liberation. What can others give you? "What is" is always here. Silence of the mind is most important. Your duty is simply *to be*: not to be "this" or "that." All that is required to realize the Self is to be still. What can be easier than that? People seem to think that by following some *practice*, the Self will someday descend upon them, giving them an experience. But the Self is realized not by *doing* something, but by refraining from doing anything— and *being* simply what one already *is*. Tranquility, in the form of silence, is bliss—that is, liberation.

Q. *To let go of the ideas "I am the body, mind, thoughts, experiences"—all of the hallmarks of the impermanent I— is what is known as surrender, right?*

R. Complete surrender is another name for liberation. Giving up what is impermanent is surrender. Find out how identification with the body takes place: body consciousness results in misery. Complete surrender means that you do not continue, in thought, as a separate entity. How could one surrender *oneself* and yet retain "individuality"? To surrender is to relinquish name-and-form thought— not to give up this and that of "my possessions." If you give up "I" and "my" instead, all is given up at a stroke. When surrender is complete, there will be no [dualistic] distinctions; one has given up one's "mind," and after that there will be no duality of any kind. Then where is the question of "my" surrendering? The "I" itself has been surrendered. Surrender is to give one's *self* up. Do not delude yourself by imagining that "you" are giving up something to "God"!

Know what real surrender means. After that, there will be no more questions. The teachings are not meant for the wise, because they do not need them. One's trouble lies with the desire to objectify. Nonattachment is the absence of both "love" and "hatred" [dualities]. Love of an *object* is of an inferior order; it cannot endure. The Self cannot be the object of love; it is itself not different from love. Realize that you are the Self.

From Dreaming to Waking

It is recorded that someone came to Ramana Maharshi and said, "I understand that you can give enlightenment."

Ramana replied: "Yes. I can give it. Can you take it?"

What is to be known, in the instance of Self-realization, is an amazing paradox. It would not be too fanciful to say that spiritual awakening can make our worldly life seem to be an optical illusion. And this is because what we're searching for, in terms of ultimate reality, has always been everything that we *see*. And that includes ourself.

As Ramana said, "Can you take it?" When the nondual teachings clarify that you (as you suppose your self to be) and the phenomenal world (that you take to be real) are illusional appearances, will you merely find that an "interesting idea"? Or, are you open to this realization radically altering your values, and the way this temporal life is lived?

All things change. Another word for change is *evolve*. The spiritual teachings, I submit, have followed a development over the centuries and continue to do so.

Naturally, from the beginning it was difficult to find words for this. A reading of the Vedic literature, Upanishads and Gitas, demonstrates the rambling attempts.

And in ancient times, for whatever murky reasons, there was a tendency to make these teachings available only in secret.

There has also been a long period of time when a seeker was required to undergo a lengthy period of testing of his sincerity before even a dialogue with a master began.

As the teachings of nonduality—which seem to have their deepest roots in the East—migrated into Western cultures, there has also been a period of attention to "translation" of words and pointers into a culturally-different idiom.

In the process of expression over centuries (and across borders), the message has been continually refined and clarified.

What has been taught even in decades past may not necessarily be the most efficacious teaching for the generally well-informed seeker of today. The format in which these teachings are presented needs to change—and will change—as there is increasing receptivity by the populace.

An increasing number of the Self-realized today have not slogged through the Vedic scriptures; undergone initiation into secret esoteric schools; performed years of manual labor for a master, to prove their commitment; sat months of silent meditation in a cold, damp cave; or solved even a single koan.

Many have simply heard the nondual teachings expounded by a seasoned exponent who is both direct and knows first-hand the Truth of which he or she speaks.

There will likely always be some seekers who will want to continue to follow older patterns of behavior in their "process." But it continues to be demonstrated that this is not necessary.

Fortunately, Buddha is not the only revered teacher who is regarded as having been enlightened. In our own time, there have been those whose life story is similarly remarkable, and whose biography and teachings are verified.

Ramana Maharshi, as a case in point (who died as recently as 1950), went from having next to nothing, to having nothing. He left his modest family home at around age 16, and chose to be homeless. He was often without even shelter, in the earlier years, before taking up lodging in a cave. When afoot, he begged for his food, and throughout his life he wore only the barest covering. He evidently never had a romantic relationship, nor did he ever travel more than a few miles from his abode near the foot of a mountain. Though an ashram was eventually formed around him, he never handled money.

The divan on which he slept and sat (while discoursing his enlightenment teachings) was in a room open to anyone, at all hours of the day. Two possessions are said to have been his, a walking stick and a water pot.

He, like Siddhartha, had surrendered every comfort, security and pleasure that most people desire. And he, too, achieved his aim of discovering the source of unending peace and contentment. And, he taught to others the means by which to do so, until he died fifty-five years after he left home. (Buddha taught for 45 years).

His teachings of nonduality are not dissimilar to those ascribed to the Buddha, but in his case we can verify the details of the accounts.

So, in terms of the sagacious teachings on the ultimate Reality, we are fortunate to not have to rely on the hearsay of millennia past.

The truths that Buddha originally promulgated have largely been corrupted by being converted into a platform for orthodoxy and doctrine: organized religion. Even more so have suffered the truths that Jesus elucidated. Within a few generations, the truths that Ramana (and some of his and our contemporaries) spoke will possibly suffer the same outcome. But, considering that there are some alive today who heard Ramana speak, his teachings concerning the ultimate are still vividly "fresh". It therefore seems wisest to concentrate one's study on this source, with reliance on what are *allegedly* Buddha's words and Jesus' words in supporting (though often unsupportable) roles.

The teachings of nonduality ("advaita": not two), written in the Vedas, are evidently the world's oldest spiritual pronouncements. They were given freshened interest several centuries ago by the historic Indian sage Shankara.

Within our era, these teachings gained world-wide attention in the presence of Ramana, who experienced spontaneous Self-realization while still in his teens—not having read the Vedas or Shankara. ("When I left home in my seventeenth year [already Self-realized]…it was only years later that I came across the term 'Brahman', when I happened to look into some books on Vedanta which had been brought to me. I was amused, and said to myself: 'Is this [condition] known as 'Brahman'?")

Ramana, at seventeen, immersed himself in several years of the deepest meditation imaginable—death-like—as he sat silent and desireless in a mountain cave. For the balance of his life, while engaged in the role of a (reluctant) guru, he owned no personal property, had no romantic life and never traveled.

Basically, he had nothing to gain from anything he said. Yet, because he personally experienced the sweeping range of human religious discovery, his teachings make it unnecessary for spiritual seekers to reinvent the wheel. Like Buddha and Jesus before him, he speaks from the authority of first-hand realization. *Unlike* Buddha and Jesus, his teachings come to us unfiltered by historic doctrinal censors.

And thankfully, for the present-day seeker, his advice is brief and direct. Ramana is deservedly the fountainhead of nondual teachings in our time.

By their fruits shall ye know them. By the lives they lived, we know the saints of enlightenment. Standing out among these, in full stature, is Ramana Maharshi. Because he lived in recent times, we have the spiritual teachings in an accurately recorded form (as compared, for example, to those of Buddha). Also, living in India, Ramana's (Tamil) words have been translated directly into English (as compared, for example, with those of Jesus: from Aramaic to Greek to Latin to English).

However, as with spiritual texts in general, discernment is required if there is to be comprehension. Such texts are un-avoidably paradoxical: what is said, at one time, from the relative standpoint, may be reiterated later from the stand-point of Absolute awareness. The irony is that this difference is best understood by the one who need not read any texts, the realized. Nevertheless, the subtle message can be comprehended by those who have the ears to hear.

The message of nondual actuality is not even dependent upon the word, as Ramana's own awakening demonstrated (and as did Buddha's). Albeit, this truth *can* be communicated with the aid of words, for those who are ready for it. The ones who are ready for it, have a single eye, and they prize what they see.

A questioner said to Ramana, "I do not know how to read. How can I realize?" Ramana said,

> "[A spiritual book] is like asking you to see yourself in a mirror. The mirror [book] reflects only what is on the face [in consciousness]. If you consult the mirror *after* washing your face [realizing Self-awareness], the face will be shown to be clean [free of confusion].
>
> "Otherwise, the mirror will indicate, 'There is dirt here [confusion]; come back after washing [clarity].'
>
> "A book does the same thing. If you read the book *after* realizing the Self, everything will be easily understood. But if you read it before realizing the Self, it will say, 'First, set yourself right; and *then* see me.'
>
> "That is all. So: *first*, know the Self!"

The problem, which besets readers of spiritual texts which speak to the unrealized reader from the realized standpoint, is in comprehending when the response is given from the relative standpoint, in comparison to when it is given from the Absolute standpoint. This can be particularly perplexing when the response is intended to show that the limited (relative) can only appear within the unlimited (Absolute) and not otherwise.

Such is the source of the unrealized reader's confusion: From the Absolute standpoint, all that can be said is "There is no thing." Ultimately, that is, the formless Absolute cannot be regarded in relation to any entity or form or object. Yet, in order to speak of this, we must speak of it as if it were something which can be identified, or objectified by the subjective hearer. Thus, it is referred to as That, or Absolute, or Formless, or God, or Self, etc.

But *this*, which necessitates being objectified in order that we can speak about it (the alternative being to remain silent, wordless), is *nothing*: no thing.

Where this becomes even more perplexing is that this *nothing* is existent in the form of—in the *appearance* of a form of—*every thing*.

To put this in context: Ramana (among others) refers to the formless Absolute as the Self—capital S. One of the (endless) forms which the Self appears *as*, is the individuated person: you; your "self". This self, being a form, is limited. Its appearance is within the Unlimited. (Even "within" is a misdirection, considering that the Formless is not an entity.)

The Unlimited being limitless, it comprises all things (which is how it can be said to appear as every thing). You appear within it. But it, being without limitation, appears in—so completely that it is *as*—you.

So, as the Unlimited appears *completely* as you, you do not have any reality as a *separate* entity (the formless Unlimited, having no point of beginning or ending, is *inseparable*). Therefore, it is said that "You do not exist."

It can be seen, by this, that it is critical to contemplate the teachings with a mind which can be fluidly open to the import of each pronouncement from both, or *either*, of the relative viewpoints (You [subject] are That [object]) *and* the Absolute perspective (there is no "You" and there is no "That"—only the unobjectifiable formless actuality).

Where the difficulty arises is that for the realized (Absolute awareness) to communicate these truths to the unrealized (with the limitation of only "relative" consciousness), the sage must, generally, speak in relative terms. But in order to show that what is being referred to is without limitations, the sage must also communicate the Absolute nature.

Where this is done effectively in a book, the bridge is there. But a bridge is inert; the explorer is responsible for the crossing.

The books that report Ramana's discussions, like other books of its kind, contains all that needs to be known by the seeker of enlightenment.

Through a piecemeal process, one tries to discover the meaning of the teachings. What I've found is that, in many cases, some element gets left out or overlooked.

The first thing I've noticed, is that people give little thought to some of the key words. The most obvious among these is a word which every spiritual tradition uses to describe the ultimate reality; omni-present.

This omnipresence is what is known as God or the Supreme Being, to some; Ramana Maharshi uses the word Self to describe it. In other words, it's not *apart* from the human self; but, at the same time, *more than*.

Whether we call it Omnipresence, God, or Self, *it* has crucial significance in how we understand "I," "you," and "world" or "reality": in other words, our life—and what is pertinent to it.

From the standpoint of a dualistic perspective, there is "I" and "others"; or, collectively, "us" and "them." The "others" and the "them" make up the "world" that "I" am in relationship with, my so-called relative "reality." It is in the context of *this* reality that our human suffering pertains. What is one to *do* about the suffering in the world, the exploitation, aggression, the turmoil?

The enlightened spiritual masters have said for millennia that the turmoil all begins with an "I"; that to be self-centered, self-interested, is basically a state of confusion, or "ignorance."

What is perceived as "my thoughts" orbit around an "individual"—separative—I. And we view these egoic thoughts as the guide for our behavior, for our every action. These "personal" thoughts are, in a word, self-serving; even the idea of "selflessness" can somehow become self-serving.

With the I-thought at the fulcrum of divisive and selfish behavior, these spiritual teachers advise us, we need to examine whether there is an alternative point of view which is more humane; *inclusive* of other "persons," rather than *exclusionary*.

This *spiritual* viewpoint, that is spoken of, is based upon a "realization of true nature" which has been intuited by perceptive people, irrespective of time or place. Its fundamental premise is that there is a universal or cosmic Presence which is free of any hinderance across time or space: infinite and eternal. As such, it is *a priori* the ground, or source, of being.

That is to say that every thing has been dependent upon this Presence; *existence* itself. Thus, as the so-called First Principle, *it* is the origination (or "creator") of our cosmos, earth, bodies, minds, thoughts, actions and their consequences; all that appears as *creation* as well as all that appears as *destruction*.

The sage views all that occurs as one unbroken movement; as a verb, be-*ing*. Celestial bodies, planets, animate and inanimate forms of life, conscious awareness, causes and their effects— this infinite and eternal *fundament* is responsible for every perplexing or paradoxical phenomenon we sense.

So this *insight*, said in the simplest way, is that every meaning that we give to something is reducible to the recognition that only one thing is ever happening: an expression of Be-ing. *Everything* is simply that one Truth. This is what is meant by "true nature."

Not everyone has come to realize true nature in a conscious way; this can be noticed, because such a realization obviates, or invalidates, the supposition that any "person" is the independent doer of the activities done; the originator of one's thoughts; or the controller of causes and effects. This lack of recognition of true nature applies to both the *individual* and the *collective*.

Therefore, coming to recognize the illusiveness of the I-thought has a relational influence on society from moment to moment. The point of the spiritual teachings is that there is no 'I' outside of, or beyond, or independent of the Self (or God, if you prefer). There are no thoughts or actions that are independent of the one omnipresent, *originating* Source. There are no activities of the world, creative or destructive, over which the individual or society has ultimate control. All of what appear to be isolated "effects" are the continuous consequence of the initiating, timeless Cause. This is what is meant by true nature.

So, an understanding of true nature will make it possible to understand what enlightened masters are saying when they speak of *non* duality, and its perspective on "you" and your "world" view.

The following statements of Ramana Maharshi will be clear, in this context:

> "All that is meant is that the Self is infinite, inclusive of all that you see. There is nothing beyond it, nor apart from it.... The source may be said to be God, or Self...If we first know the Self, then all other matters will be plain to us....

> "Intellect (thinking) is only an instrument of the Self.... There is only one Consciousness.... [Thoughts] arise from the Self.... Mind (otherwise) does not exist.... The mind is only a projection from the Self. The Self continues to exist in the absence of the mind...(but mind) cannot exist apart from the Self.... 'Your' mind, and intellect (thoughts), are the factors of your wrong identity ('I').... Give up this mistaken identity, and... Self will be seen to be the single, nondual Reality.... For a realized being, the Self *alone* is the reality."

The true nature of the thinker of thoughts is the Self. The true nature of the doer of all deeds is likewise the Self. "Do not think that you are the doer.... [The actions] are not your own. They are God's activities.... Let us not pose as the doers."

To those who take the view of being somehow apart from, or independent of, the Self, "other individuals" will likewise be viewed as additional objects, to the object called "me." And as "me" and "others" are conceived to be separate objects, so too the "world" will be seen as yet an additional "part" of "objective reality."

What we suppose we see as an objective, or independent, world is essentially a separative or dualistic *thought*. Thoughts have their source in the Self. The conceived "individual" self is, in its true nature, the ever-present Self. When the 'I' comes to recognize its true nature, this Self-realized being then looks out upon "others" and the activities in the "world" and sees everywhere only its indivisible Self.

Ramana counsels:

> "You are not instructed to shut your eyes from the *world*. You are only to *see* your 'self' first, and then see the whole world as the Self."

Thus, for those who ask, "What is to be done about conditions in the world?," Ramana replies:

> "First set yourself right, and *then only* set out to improve 'others'. Change the *hearts* of men and the *world* will surely change. But one must begin somewhere; and one can begin only with oneself."

Ramana's teaching was that the Self (Absolute) alone is. There is not anything which that is not, therefore it is in no way *apart* from anything. Though this is so, we do not automatically recognize that our fundamental condition is that we are in essence none other than That.

It is this Absolute by which "all that is" is manifest. Among the manifestations are the human organism, its brain, its sense organs, the thoughts which arise, the mind which is comprised of these thoughts, and the ego by which the organism declares "*I see.*"

It is this ego—self identification—which constructs the subject-object duality: me, and that which I do not perceive as me. Though this separative bias seemingly causes us to view the subject *I* as dissociated from anything which is not recognized as the body-brain-mind-ego, it is in fact nothing more than another manifested product of the omnipresent Self.

You—all elements and aspects of you, including the ego which posits otherwise—are only the Self. When this is clearly realized, it is realized that there *is* no individual ego (*all* egos, as is everything else, are the same Self), and the subject-object bias disintegrates. There is then recognized to be but one thing—the seer which sees no "other," separate object. This *Self*-realization has been the condition of the jnani throughout the ages, expressed at least 3,500 years ago as Tat Tvam Asi: That Thou Art. (*Whatever* "that" is.)

Ramana focuses on the self-awareness, which each seeker has, of his/her own existence. That very existence is essential to the Self. Our true nature, or identity, can be summarized as "I am." Anything which follows, or is added on to that, is merely another extension or elaboration of the Self: e.g., "I am the doer"; the *Self* is the doer. "I am the thinker"; the *Self* is the thinker.

Ramana utilized particular ways in which to attempt to bring the seeker to recognize his/her underlying essence. (And on some rare occasions, the seed of realization was obviously planted, as evidenced by the listener confirming having gotten the point.)

For example, in our relative, human condition, it could be said that there are three different but connected levels of consciousness: what we consider to be our "normal" condition, when our eyes are open and we are wide awake and in relationship to the "real world"; when our eyes are closed and our body in repose, yet the thinking, imaginative mind is still functioning in support of our discriminating ego, and we are acting in relationship to an acknowledged unreal "dream world"; and when consciousness has sunk beneath the stage of thought and ego identification, and we are in a deep, death-like, "unconscious" condition, dream-free and thought-free. The connecting thread in all of these varied, cyclical conditions is consciousness; if consciousness ceased to be present in any of these three conditions, the life cycle would end.

While consciousness is the underlying and connecting presence in all three conditions, it varies in its manifest form in each. In the awake state, it is the substratum on which the ego interacts with material elements and phenomenon considered to exist objectively in time and space. In the dreaming phase, it is the screen upon which the mind plays images and possibilities, free of the constraints of limiting time, space or cause-and-effect. In the period of deep sleep, consciousness exists free of the imposition of cognitive thought and interpreted sense impressions; pure empty awareness with no "real" or "unreal" object envisioned. This aspect of unadulterated, unconditioned consciousness is our absolute essence, the common and unitary presence at the core of each and *every one* of us.

Since this indiscriminate presence is our *fundament* at every moment, it is permanent and unchanging. It is our true Self, upon which our changing self—and its consequent thoughts, emotions, actions, etc.—are passing, inconsequent phenomena.

In deep sleep, we neither affirm nor deny our existence; we simply are—as (and what) we are—without any identification or I-centeredness and also without any idea of objective phenomenon, either "real" or "unreal." The "world"—and every "other" thing—is nonexistent in this presence. When we *recognize* our essence (in our waking state), the false identification as a separate I dissolves. This is Self-*realization*, plain and simple.

You needn't be confused by some of the terminology, in the writings concerning Advaita. All of the "many names for God" are—despite their origin in different cultures—pointing ultimately to the same One, the same Absolute, the infinite and eternal omnipresence that is considered to be the ground of all being.

Ramana, for example, uses the word Self (with a capital S) to denote the Absolute. The reason for this is because he is trying to emphasize that the "you"—the "self" with the small s—is, in essence, the very same Self.

Some writers, in Vedanta, use the word *Brahman* rather than *Self*, but again both words equate with the Absolute.

Then again, the word *Consciousness*—as in "cosmic Consciousness"—is also sometimes used; usually capitalized, to make clear that the allusion is not to the limited sense of consciousness (as "awareness") that the self supposes that it possesses "individually."

And then there's what Ramana calls the "false I"—the sense that the subjective "person" embodies some sort of separate entity—which predicates the "I-versus-you" dichotomy. Thus when he speaks of the "true I" of course, he means your essential nature as an aspect of the Absolute—in which the I/you perspective disappears.

Adding to the confusion, Ramana sometimes also uses the word *Heart*—not meaning the organ you call the heart, but rather the "center" or essence of your being (in the dictionary distinction: "the central, vital or main part; core"). He sometimes calls this "the cave of the Heart." In all cases, he means to designate the Absolute.

And, like others, he occasionally speaks of the "light," a word which for centuries has been an equivalent for Absolute presence.

So, the point is that as you encounter these myriad, generalized descriptive terms simply read them as merely alternate names for the Absolute. There need be no confusion whatever if you bear this consistently in mind.

Also: do not ever lose sight of the fact that an intellectual (or scholarly) understanding of what is written will not, of itself, result in enlightenment.

What *will* result in enlightenment is when the seeker herself dissolves into the Absolute omnipresence. In other words, as long as there is a "self" which is in search of the

Absolute, duality will persist. What is infinitely and eternally omnipresent need not be searched for: it, pervading all things, cannot even be *avoided*; it is present *as* all that *is* present, saturating even the seeker herself—thus *non*-dual.

That is *why* Ramana makes the point, the self *is* the Self: there is but one actuality.

Put another way, "cosmic" Consciousness and "your" very own moment-to-moment consciousness are not separate. In Buddhism, they use the word Mind (capital M) for Absolute "consciousness" to make the point (like Ramana's Self/self) that this universal Mind is the same as "your" sense of being imbued with a mind (small m). It's just that your *idea* of mind is limited, rather than (as with the enlightened) unlimited. Remove the limits you construe for the self, and you discover that there can *only* be the Self.

Ramana uses the attribution "Self" in the same way that other teachers use the word Absolute. He wants you to understand that your *true* "self" is not different than the Self.

But the true self which Ramana points to, your Absolute self, has no characteristics. You might conclude that you are insufficient in this quality or that quality, but your Absolute nature is beyond the limitations of any quality. Qualities— pro or con—are a concoction of your mind.

In other words, your beingness as Self is not dependent upon whether you are adjudged to be an adequate person or an inadequate person. A rose with five petals is not less of a rose than one with twenty-four petals. The Self is all that is, as

Ramana says. The Self, then, constitutes the inadequate as well as the adequate.

Probably the best organized sourcebook of Ramana's teachings is *Be As You Are,* compiled by David Godman in 1985 from two dozen written accounts. Running some 200 pages, it's divided into six general topics with a seven-page glossary and five pages of index.

Ramana has said, "Somehow it never occurs to me to write any book, or compose poems." Yet he very occasionally did both, briefly, when requested by devotees. English translations of five texts, plus various verses, are available in *The Collected Works of Ramana Maharshi,* assembled by Arthur Osborne in 1972. This book, of about 200 pages, has an eight-page glossary and four-page index.

Talks with Sri Ramana Maharshi contains some 650 brief, transcribed Q-and-A's on many topics (with students or with visitors) over about four years in the late 1930's. 640 pages, hardcover, with extensive glossary and index, it is best read with the above preparation. A thorough Bibliography, at the back, will lead you to choices of the many other books, of many sorts, to read after.

Now in its 13th printing since publication in 1955, *Talks with Sri Ramana Maharshi* was produced by Maharshi's ashram in India. From 1935-39, a disciple acted as a recorder of Maharshi's dialogues with visitors—somewhat like journal entries. Maharshi was evidently well-read in classical Indian spiritual literature (*after* his enlightenment), so—in speaking frequently to Indians—he often used Sanskrit phrases.

While earlier editions of the book had only a 10-page glossary, and a 24-page general index, it now has a 42-page index—with each Sanskrit indexed word followed, at the same location, with its definition. In addition, there are 33 pages of categorized indexes to assist in locating a passage you only recall, making it a more useuful resource. Otherwise, it's the same, original text.

Sri is an honorific, similar to Sir; *Bhagavan* is a title given to holy persons, similar to Blessed. Devotees referred to Sri Bhagavan Ramana Maharshi simply as Bhagavan; the book uses "M," as an abbreviation for Maharshi.

Ramana was about in his mid-50's during this time. The significance of his life and teaching is that spiritual aspirants need not reinvent the wheel. In terms of spiritual experience, it is evident (as one can recognize in reading a biography of Maharshi) that he has "been there, and done that." Among the visitors, just during these four years, were Somerset Maugham, Yogananda, Tibetan scholar Evans-Wentz, writer Paul Brunton, Maurice Frydman (compiler of Nisargadatta's *I Am That)*, swamis, muslims, the Maharajahs of Mysore and of Travancore, Indian congressmen, Brahmin pandits, and philosophy professors.

Among the many that sat in his presence each day were those caught up in the traditional concepts of established religions (Hindu, Christian, Muslim, Buddhist, Theosophy, etc.)—such as 'reincarnation'. Then there were the scholars who treat enlightenment as an academic subject and want to clarify scriptural terms. There are, of course, those who come in quest of occult and mystical powers. And there are inevitably those who appear with a "problem"—men and women alike.

There are many who want instant dispensation ("grace"; shaktipat), by the guru tapping their forehead or whispering a mantra in their ear, as if being enlightened by an ATM machine.

Practically every entreaty could be summarized, "Tell me, what is realization? And how may I attain it?" Since the listener usually resists thinking "outside the box," his teaching is plain, simple and direct; the listener—who would like as long as possible to continue in his or her worldly ways—often ignores his direction and asks instead if Ramana can recommend some "practice" that can be pursued toward the same ends "meanwhile."

Ramana is realistically pragmatic. He judges the state of spiritual maturity of his listener (often by the question) and responds accordingly. Answers are always keyed to the level of the listener's comprehension. If a person insists on asking about karma, Ramana begins by quoting some of the things that are said in the spiritual literature about karma—but which are invariably misunderstood. He may then comment pointedly, "Karma is as real as the *individual*."

His responses are almost predictably repetitive, because he had one succinct message. And generally he used the term "Self" (which the scribe capitalized) to refer to the Absolute, to stress the point that absolute *Self* is the same as the *self*—individual—with a small "s". But he also used "Brahman" with Hindus, "God" with Christians, etc. And he sometimes used "I-I," indicating the One "I" that is at the *same time* the individual I.

He generally spoke in reference to himself as a *Jnani*, which defines a Self-realized sage. Its counterpart, a person who has not realized his true nature, is an *ajnani* (a- indicating "not").

The idea that there exists in reality a separate entity (*any* separate entity), such as "I," is to miss the point to which the nondual sages are alluding.

Ramana's favorite expiation is to establish three "states" (even though they are not separate from each other) of our consciousness: when we are awake (alert to the "external" world); when we are dreaming (cognitive of, and identified with, the non-external fantasizing of the psyche); and that of deep sleep.

In deep sleep, consciousness continues; but without any reference to the "external world" or the "internal world": no identification with either extrapolation, as (otherwise) when awake or dreaming...consciousness with no self-identification (I, me, my) involved.

This "pure" aware presence is what Ramana (and others) refers to as our "true nature"; before anything whatsoever is added to it: no *self-identification* has been imposed on it. "You" are *missing* from it.

In this condition, there are no separate entities, because in this condition the separative thought process is non-existent. Here, there can be no "dreams" (object) nor "dreamer" (subject).

Here, there is not "enlightenment," nor any "person" to be enlightened. There is nothing missing, because there is "nothing from the start" to which anything could be added or subtracted.

Ramana's injunction to "ask yourself, 'who am I?'" is considered by many to be his most important teaching. It's importance is in inducing the questioner to investigate "what is the *source* of the presumed *entity* which is asking the question?" (or any question, for that matter). The immediate source of any question—of all speculation, in fact—is the thought, the idea, that there *is* an "I" to pose the question: the innocent question "who *am* I?" can open the door to the provocative question "*Is* there an I?" Or is the "I" simply another thought form, as are any questions in association with it?

Ramana points out that during the period of deep sleep, we are "dead to the world". Self-referenced imaging ceases: we are not aware of our self—or any self or non-self—nor any other thing, or any conceived relationship between things. In this condition, the question "who am I?" is automatically self-resolved.

Yet, there is a being—or rather, beingness—present: were one to be shaken by another's hand, waking consciousness would reappear as certainly as if it had never been absent.

What "you" truly are, then, in your primal form, is that which gives rise to—or creates—all that is known to the I, including its self. "You", in your purest beingness, are not "I"; you are the source of the I—and all else which ostensibly is perceived by that presumed entity.

Ramana would say that *this* "you" is a "permanent" condition, therefore ever-actual or "real". The "I" comes and goes, dying (daily) in its dream and waking states into its persistent dreamless condition; so the I is impermanent (being recreated daily) and is therefore *not* real, a phantasm.

What makes this (deeper) understanding of Ramana's teaching so important is that it is an unerring graveyard for the stubborn I-thought. Whenever a perplexity arises to the cognitive "self", Ramana would advise reflecting: "Did this dilemma arise during deep sleep?" No. Therefore, it is a non-real, a phantasmic, dilemma.

Did the question "who am I?" arise in deep sleep? No. Therefore, if you understand "who" you are in deep sleep, you need not concern yourself about it—or any other thought-generated concern, for that matter.

So, even more fruitful than asking your "self" who-am-I?, is the one-pointed reflection "Did this thought occur in deep sleep?" This reflection will silence the I-generated conflicts.

"You" and "me" are impermanent forms; all such forms come and go. There is a Presence in which all forms arise, and into which they will disappear; this Presence does not come and go.

Ramana has put it this way: that which does not come and go, which is eternal or everlasting, is the only thing which is "real"; all else is "unreal," merely a passing appearance.

All forms—e.g., you and me—owe their original "identity" to this ground of Being. So, from the standpoint of ultimate *reality*, who are *you*? Who am I? What difference is there, in that context?

That is what is meant by, "There is nobody," no "thing" or entity. Therefore, one comes to realize that there is no "me." And, given that realization, there are no "others."

This is not to say that the *appearance* of a me and others even needs to be absent. The realization involves recognizing "who," or "what," these are appearances (or manifestations) *of.* That (Beingness) thou art—*thou* applying to you, me and all others.

One of the things which makes spiritual traditions mystical is their concurrence on the paradoxical aspect of revelation.

We believe the world and its objects to be real. How is it said that they are *unreal*?

Put another way, most people have no doubt that the material manifestations are real, but have great doubt as to whether the presence of the Absolute is real.

That which is real, in the context of the sages, is *always* real—unchanged throughout eternity. All that is created and destroyed—even primordial solar systems—are *not* real.

All that is impermanent comes and goes, in the context of a backdrop that is *without* beginning or ending. An analogy that has been given is that of the progression of movie footage on a *screen*, which supports the activity without movement on its own part.

In the case of universal manifestation, the background is without form, whereas all things which appear as contrast on the background *have* form, and each 'thing' is *limited* to its form.

Since the unlimited formless is what is fundamentally real, it has to be the *ground* which gives rise—en potentia—to all that is materially manifest.

In other words, the forms are dependent upon the formless for their arising; the impermanent exists on a lattice of the permanent.

But, just as the 'unreal' cannot exist without the real, the real has no *appearance* of existence without the unreal. The formless has no *existence* objectively, without taking form.

The impermanent things are the forms through which the formless experiences its reality. They are the *immanent* presence of the *transcendent* presence ("God's *image*").

"You," as an individual, are one of the unreal forms superimposed on the backdrop of the real. As a *manifestation* of the formless, you are not *separate* from the formless; the real and the unreal, being inseparable, are in actuality simply one whole, complete actuality; so you are not entirely *un*real.

The unreal cannot *appear* to our consciousness without the *existence* of the real. The formless Real is not merely a presence *around* the unreal; it is a real presence in and *through* all that is.

All that we see can be viewed as Real or unreal, depending on the perspective: "half full, or half empty." But the point is: *both; not two.*

That tree is real. And it is unreal. It surpasses either category. Your body-mind is unreal; your formless presence is unchangingly real.

Ramana:

"Shankara says

Brahman is real;

the Universe is unreal;

Brahman is the Universe...."

Ramana explains:

"The Universe is conceived to be apart from Brahman [by the unenlightened], and that perception is wrong....

"A mirage does not *disappear*, even after one's knowing it to be a mirage: the *envisioned* is still there—but the person does not run to it for water....The world is an illusion. Even after knowing that, it continues to appear. It must be known to be *Brahman*, and not apart.

"If the world appears, *to whom* does it appear...the Self. Otherwise, would the world appear in the *absence* of the Self? Therefore, the Self, is the reality. The phenomena are real [only] *as the Self*; and are illusions [when] *apart from* the Self....That is what is meant by 'reality and unreality' being one and the same....

"A phenomenon cannot be a reality simply because it serves a [practical] purpose. Take a dream, for example; they serve a purpose.

"Dream *water* quenches dream *thirst*. The dream creation, however, is contradicted in the waking state.

"The waking creation ["real world"] is contradicted in the other two states [while in a dream, or in deep sleep]....If real, a thing must *ever* be real; and not real for a short time and unreal at other times....

"Similarly, the universe cannot be real of itself: that is to say, apart from the *underlying* Reality."

Asked what is the major lesson of the spiritual teachings, I'd have to say that it is *impermanence*.

As Ramana Maharshi points out, all forms (whether material or immaterial) arise then dissipate; they are impermanent. The actuality in which they originate and subside is infinite and eternal, and is itself without form. Thus, this ground of being is the only element which is not impermanent. Ultimately, as Ramana says, this Being-ness is the only lasting reality.

In Buddhism, it is emphasized that "all *things* change." That formless reality, which is not one of the nameable things, and which is not limited by time or space, is the Unchanging.

The spiritual teachings urge us to focus attention on what is permanent and ever present (which Ramana would call *real*), rather than on the ephemeral, the fleeting forms (which Ramana calls *unreal*).

The ultimate reality is said to be the source of all that is; and, as such, is what all the relative things hold in common. What the enlightened masters perceive is *sameness*, the essence which links "the ten thousand things" in unity, Oneness. The sage perceives this indivisible essence as one's true nature. It was "your face before you were born"; your form appeared in this empty presence, and will disappear into it—the ground of being remaining entirely unaffected. From the standpoint of the Ultimate, each "individual life" is meaningless.

The recognition of impermanence places petty, self-generated concerns in their proper perspective. It leaves attention undistracted, to contemplate each unsecured moment in awareness that it may be the viewer's last.

Pick up a newspaper any day, and you'll read about someone who walked out their front door that morning and never returned. Nonexistence for an organism may be only one breath away. You might rinse your wine glass this evening and never fill it again.

Paul Krassner once told me, "The central fact of my life is my death." To live one's life not taking any of its conditions complacently for granted is to appreciate the presence which is manifest. It is, as Krishnamurti titled one of his books, *A Wholly Different Way of Living*. It is to have incorporated the teachings regarding impermanence.

If, despite appearances, there is no "self" in reality, what is "inhabiting" this body?

What is it that concerns itself with such distinctions as "real," opposed to "unreal"? What becomes of that discerning intellect when the unanimated body is finally just so-many pounds of inert flesh?

As Ramana would say, the body is a real as *you* are. At some point, the "you" will disappear, and the "reality" of the body— in fact, all bodies—will disappear along with it.

What remains, then, must be *really* real. What, in that case, will concern itself with whatever has appeared in our analytic consciousness?

Ramana's means of pointing to the essential truth was to reiterate that, in actuality, not anything is permanently or finally existent but the Self. All things come and go in the Self; therefore all but the Self is not genuine or truly existent. When this truth is clearly perceived, the "I-thought" (the idea of self existence—for anything other than the Essence) falls away: no longer a "personal" psyche identifying with a particular organism.

Where there is no longer an 'individual' self in awareness, there is no longer the idea or concept of a self's 'body,' 'mind' or 'thoughts'. Anything which can be named is merely an alias for one thing: that Essence.

That is why, when a visitor complained that his "mind wandered", Ramana's reply was: "Is there a mind?"

"If the enquiry is made whether mind exists", said Ramana, "it will be found that mind does not exist. That is [how to affect] 'control of the mind.'"

To another questioner, he said: "You can never find the mind through mind. Pass beyond it, in order to find it non-existent."

Someone suggested, "The mind must kill the mind."

Ramana: "Yes, if there be the mind. A search for it discloses its non-existence. How can anything that does not exist be killed?"

If there is no existent mind, then there are no thoughts, either, existent in actuality.

Q. "Then thoughts are not real?"

R. "They are not: the only reality is the Self."

Only Essence exists. Ramana liked to point out that it is as Essence that we exist when the body is un-conscious. "What is your experience in deep sleep? There were no thoughts, no mind; and yet you remained then."

Ramana would proceed to point out that all that we conceive —all the named things and phenomena—are merely manifestations of Essence, or Self.

> "Mind is one form of manifestation of life.... The vital force manifests as life-activity and also as the conscious phenomena known as the mind....If the inquiry into the ultimate cause of manifestation of mind itself is pushed, mind will be found to be only the manifestation of the Real, which is otherwise called Atman or Brahman."

At another time: "Mind is only the dynamic power of the Self." [In Buddhism, what Ramana refers to as Self, with a capital S, is referred to as Mind, with a capital M.]

> "If one realizes that thoughts arise from the Self, and abides in their source, the mind will disappear....In their absence, there is neither the world nor God the Creator [as conceived]."

Thoughts are a manifestation of that Essence which cannot be conceived:

> "Now, what about thoughts?...Where from do they arise? Their source, ever-present and not subject to variations, must be admitted to be. It must be the Eternal state, as said."

Clarifying further:

> "There is no entity by name of 'mind.' Because of the emer-gence of thoughts, we surmise some thing from which they start: that we term mind. When we probe to see what it is,

there is nothing like it. After it has 'vanished,' Peace will be found to remain eternal."

The idea that there is such an isolated entity as mind, or thought, is a self-generated idea, an idea that follows on the heels of the "I-thought"—independent existence. "Thoughts cannot exist but for the ego."

Q. "How may one destroy the mind?"

R. "Is there a mind, in the first place? What you call mind is an illusion. It starts from the I-thought."

Further:

> "After the emergence of the mind, the universe appears and the body is seen to be 'contained' in it. Whereas, all these are contained in the Self, and they cannot exist apart from the Self....

> "Its [mind] destruction is the non-recognition of it as being apart from the Self. Even now the mind is not. Recognize it!....It is not real, but a phantom proceeding from the Self. That [recognition] is how the mind is destroyed!"

Ramana's summation:

> "The individual confines himself to the limits of the changeful body or of the mind—which derives its existence from the unchanging Self. All that is necessary is to give up this mistaken identity; and, that done, the ever-shining Self will be seen to be the single non-dual Reality."

Ramana Maharshi's teaching is that the Self (Absolute) alone is. There is not anything which that is not, therefore it is in no way *apart* from anything. Though this is so, we do not automatically recognize that our fundamental condition is that we are in essence none other than that.

As That (of which all that is, is manifest), among the manifestations are the human organism, its brain, its sense organs, the thoughts which arise, the mind which is comprised of these thoughts, *and* the ego by which the organism declares "I think."

It is this ego—self identification—which constructs the subject-object duality: me, and that which I do not perceive as me. Though this separative bias stands as an obstacle which seemingly causes us to view the subject I as dissociated from anything which is not recognized as the body-brain-mind-ego, it is in fact nothing more than another manifested product of the omnipresent Self.

Once the awakening process is underway, one begins to re-examine, in a new light, that which heretofore had been perceived in duality.

The central point of nonduality is that there is only one recognition that you need to be continually conscious of, and that will be the key to all that you need to know. It is this: all that *is* (everything, whether we say it is existent or non-existent), is the one single, indivisible actuality. Any thing which is formed, formless, named or unnamable is, in the final analysis, that illimitable actuality in essence.

Confusingly, this all-inclusive actuality has been identified in a plethora of ways, over mankind's history. As just a few: God, Absolute, That, Self, He. Ultimately, it makes no difference what *name* is given to *anything*, since *all* things are merely expressions of the fundamental actuality.

However, due to our ingrained dualistic mindset, it is important to give some attention (at least initially) to this matter of referential wording concerning this underlying actuality. Consider for yourself whether some referential wording may not be more likely to lend itself to dualistic reverberations than others. Some, for example, have historically been associated with a dualistic conception of an entity that is inevitably viewed as apart from the viewer himself: He/Him, Lord, and God are examples of these, and the separative (dualistic) conception involved is clearly depicted on Michelangelo's ceiling in the Sistine Chapel; the anthropomorphic Jehovah— of whom the Bible speaks of his face, eyes, ears, hands, and his sitting and standing.

Even the Eastern term Self risks carrying a connotation of something similar to "my" self, which I think of as having a "mind" and intentions and plans, and so on.

For this reason, much of the classical Advaita writings utilize a more neutral term, such as That; however, even such a word leaves us with a choice that might better be regarded as *This*.

A more definitive choice, and one which is found consistently throughout all spiritual source works, is the word Absolute. So, too, the word Omnipresent.

But regardless of which term you feel comfortable with, it can be helpful to focus your attention on *one* referential term for the *one* actuality. This avoids such confusion, for example, as considering that "God is a part of the Absolute." Or such conceptions as "the Absolute is His expression." Or He/Self, Self/God, etc., which are subliminally dualistic expressions. *All* that is (by *whatever* name), is that *One* singular actuality. "Self" *is* the Absolute. "God" *is* the Absolute. "He" is the Absolute. (Or, Omnipresent—or whatever *singular* term you choose to confine your reference to.)

This expression, for example—"The Absolute must move within Self [God] if God [Self] is the All"—might be stated:

"The Absolute *must* 'move' within the Absolute, if the Absolute is all that there *is*."

And this makes it clear that, ultimately, there is not *even* "movement" as a *separate* distinction *apart* from the Absolute. All that is (movement included) is merely the Absolute in its actual expression.

Or, as you recognized it, "This [the Absolute] is motion*less*." This consistent awareness of the overarching nondual actuality causes you to avoid such ingrained dualistic conceptions as "cause" and "effect." The Absolute *being* all that is, it would have to be *both* all possible causes *and* all potential effects. Put another way, where there is nothing *but* a singular actuality, cause and effect are meaningless, separative distinctions.

How much more simple (and effective) a key could we be given than to recognize, "*All* that *is*, is That"—and to be finished in one sweep with confusion and division?

This is what "clarity" means—clear, no obstructions!

Three statements by Ramana:

"The Absolute is the Self. It is God."

"The Self is God."

"The Self is the Absolute..."

(Did he contradict himself? Or is *all* One?)

Vedanta, generally speaking, is the organized study (and/or interpretation) of the ancient Indian collection of spiritual literature known as the Vedas. A part of the Vedas, the Upanishads (possibly dating between 800-600 B.C.) describe a form of spiritual liberation that is called yoga; among the various yogas is *jnana*, which leads to samadhi—immersion of the self into the all-encompassing fundamental reality (called Brahman, or the Self). These (Sanskrit) scriptures were evidently secret, at one time.

A particular emphasis in Vedanta, known as Advaita, was the focus of Adi Shankara, renowned in India as a teacher circa 800 A.D. He stressed that the Vedas declare that Brahman is the all-pervading, nondual essence that animates every self.

Advaita Vedanta (or jnana yoga) is best known in modern times as the life teaching of the Indian ascetic Ramana Maharshi, who died in 1950; his theme was that the Self which you seek to be united with is already your own essential self.

Ramana's teachings actually went further than Advaita; they reflected the most refined form of Advaita, which is called Ajata. Basically, Advaita emphasizes that "All is One"; Ajata erases both the "All" and the "One" as definitional concepts. Any thoughts of "existence" are dependent upon sensate consciousness; the dead are devoid of both the ideational entities of the Self or of the self.

So, the teachings of Ramana reflect the "emptiness" or "void" of reality, which renders all analytical philosophies moot.

Adi Shankara systematized the Vedic teachings and traveled around India, debating the Brahmin priests (whom he argued had ritualized and corrupted the tenets which the writings implied).

The codifying of these enlightenment teachings is what we know today as *advaita*, which means "not two", or nonduality. There is but one constant actuality, in other words, and its essence unifies *all* things as One.

Enlightenment is considered to be the personal realization that nonduality is the ultimate truth of the nature of each of us. However, in the initial stages of this realization, the perceiver tends to think in terms of *enlightenment* versus *non-enlightenment*; in a subtle way, a dualistic distinction.

Ramana states that he taught *ajata*, the most fundamental distillation of advaita. This word means "no creation": it goes beyond even such distinctions as *duality* or *nonduality*, and even *existence* and *non-existence*; in other words, "not *two* [duality], not *one* [nonduality]", and can be summed up–as in Hui Neng's poem—"If there is nothing from the start, where can the dust [or any existing "thing"] alight?"

So, the "basic" condition of the ultimate actuality is no-*thing*ness, or nothingness; also describable as "emptiness", or in Buddhism "the void". As Buddha states in the Diamond

Sutra, "no beginning is the highest truth", and he speaks of the "birthless nature" of reality—"an illusion...a bubble, a dream...view all created *things* like this."

The condition of ajata, emptiness, is the condition which the word enlightenment intends finally to point out; and when it is seen that one's own life is empty (as Buddha indicates of his own, in the Diamond Sutra), this is what is described as the "highest state", sahaja samadhi. The awakened one lives from the place of emptiness, or "no creation, from the start".

When teachers, such as Ramana, speak of being "asleep while awake", what is meant is a mind (in the waking state) which is "empty" of concepts, ideas, expectations, evaluations, conflicts, et cetera, as the mind in our deep, dreamless sleep.

The metaphor of being asleep while awake is analogous to the dictum to "be like an infant"; attentive to the immediate present rather than past or future, and an absence of ideals, conjecture, ambition, and so on.

These are colorful ways of speaking of an awareness which is not caught up in the usual concerns of the world.

Muruganar quotes Ramana: "all this external, material universe is unreal.... There is nothing other than [the Self]." All entities, limited and impermanent, are "false appearances" when not viewed to be merely shimmers of the (unlimited and permanent) Absolute. Because the formless Absolute is difficult to envision, cultures often assign a form and a name to it: for example, God.

Our idea of "creation" is just *that*—an *idea* about something. For there to be creation, as such, there would have to be an *intent* to create. A "God" might be said to have an intent; but the formless Absolute has no need of *intentions*, since there can be nothing in opposition to it.

Ramana explains about God as an entity or form:

> "The process that brings 'the world' into existence [relative consciousness] simultaneously brings Iswara [God] into 'being'....But this is only true from the *relative* standpoint of those who have not realized the truth...From the *Absolute* standpoint, the *sage* [in Consciousness] cannot accept any *other* existence than the *impersonal* Self, one and formless....

> "The forms and names of God are many and various, and differ with each religion. *Its* essence is the same as ours, the real Self being one, and without form. Hence, forms it *assumes* [such as in consciousness, or imagination—a word relating to "image"] are only [self-] creations or *appearances*."

> "God, the Creator, the personal God, is the last of the unreal *forms* to go [in order to awaken]. *Only* the Absolute being is *real*. Hence not only the world, not only the ego [self], but also the personal 'God' are of *unreality*."

If only the Self (Absolute) is real, then all else is unreal— including the self ("me"). For the ajnani (unenlightened), it is the relative consciousness which creates (or, in which arises) all separations, all entities (limited, impermanent), all forms— including the form of "me," or "I." Then this (divided) I looks out on what it envisions as a (divided) "world."

The jnani looks out and sees *only* the Absolute. *And* for the jnani it is not "I" doing the looking—it is the Absolute. His eyes are the Absolute's eyes, and all that can be seen is the Absolute.

Godman: "This Infinite eye sees and knows nothing other than *itself*, and it accomplishes this without the *false division* of 'seer' and 'seen'."

The Absolute is only—and always—"seeing" itself.

Ramana:

> "First [on initial awakening] one sees the Self as objects ["The world is the Self!"]; then one sees the Self as a void ["I am the Self—and the Self is no-thing!"]; only in this last state [complete Self-*realization*] there is no seeing... There is no "me" as "the seer." There is only "the one who sleeps [body] without sleeping [Absolute]."

> "Only that stage is final where there is no 'seeing'... no seer, seeing and *object* [that is "apart" from the Absolute seer] to see. What exists then is *only* the Infinite eye [the eye as merely another aspect of the Absolute]....The real Eye is the Self....

> "If you realize you are without form, that you are unlimited, that you *alone* exist...what is there to be seen 'apart'?...if the Self alone exists, it is *both* 'seer' *and* 'seen'—and above [beyond] 'seeing', or being seen....There is nothing *apart* from the Self."

If you *understand* these pages, you understand the fundament of Ramana's enlightenment teachings.

So, you ask, what is one to say about bhakti ("devotion, worship"); or prayer?

Worship can only persist, as Ramana says, "so long as there is a sense of separation." One is only truly *devoted* when one has merged one's "self" into the Absolute. "Then," Ramana says, "*Who* is the worshipper? The answer is: the Self."

Likewise, he says, "There must be an 'I' who prays. If 'God's Will be done,' why pray at all? There is no necessity to let *Him* know your needs: God doesn't require an intermediary. God is *in* all, and works *through* all."

What did Ramana say about *sadhana* ("path"); that is, "practice" such as meditation? "People seem to think that by practicing some elaborate sadhana, the Self would one day descend upon them.... Sadhana implies an object to be *gained*, and the means of *gaining* it.... *I* had no rules of meditation or contemplation. Mediation is possible only if the ego be kept up."

In other words, the aspirants' idea is that "if I do some procedure, process or ritual correctly, and if I do it long enough, I will come in contact with ultimate Reality": it will someday "descend upon them."

The irony is that the presence of ultimate Reality—ever-present everywhere at all times—not only surrounds the meditator (whether or not meditating), and in fact imbues— is the very essence of—every meditator or non-meditator. There is nowhere you can go, and nothing you can do, that can ever bring you "closer" to That (or Self) than you are in any moment.

This is precisely why the teachings say "there is nothing to *get*; you *are* what you are seeking!" The seeker supposes herself to be some thing other than That, and That to be the *object* which one will encounter. This is what in Buddhism, is called a "gaining idea": *I*, subject, will somehow *gain* (or come into possession of) *It* (or knowledge of It: "enlightenment"), the object of my pursuit in time.

The subject, supposing that she's separate from the Self she seeks, is still regarding herself as an "individual," an independent entity. This *person-al* identification is what Ramana is referring to as the ego. Only as long as this *individual* identification is maintained can the self *not* be realized to be the Self she would propose to "encounter." All she would need to do is, one time, get to the bottom of the query Ramana phrases as "who (or what) *am* 'I'?" The *seers'* answer is, That, the Self.

Were the meditator to recognize that all activity (such as meditating, or not meditating) is an inadvertent expression of the omnipresent Self, she would comprehend that the "two"—the Self, and all activity which is a manifest expression of it—are merely aspects of the same singular actuality. The pointlessness of meditating as a *means* to an *end* is as apparent as this: any *activity* that is reflected in a mirror (by "individuals") is not independent of the mirror (ultimate Reality). To presume that the meditator could somehow ever be apart from ultimate Reality is obviously a dualistic distinction which leads *away* from the recognition of "oneness."

"...Realize the pure, *undifferentiated* being of the Self, or Absolute....

"'Intentional' meditation involves a subject who has some objective.... You must learn to realize all 'subject' and 'object' as *one*; and in the *meditating*, you are destroying that sense of oneness—and creating duality....When the sense of separateness is lost, and the *objective* of meditation along with the *subject* who meditates is left behind—without anything else to know—it is Realization.... The Realized has *become* the Self, and there is nothing more to do.... *This* is enlightenment."

When the seeking thus ends, the seeker has understood that there is not anything she needs to do, or practice, in order to *be* the Self which has (amusingly) been sought. To be as you *are* is to be the Self! One's *self*-identity is recognized as the *Self's* identity: undifferentiated.

> "No aids are needed to know one's own Self; that is, to be aware.... Liberation is only to *remain* aware of the Self. No long process is necessary to know the Self.... I am saying that the Self is self-evident.... Why do you wish to meditate at all?... Why do you not remain as you are without meditating?... Self is realized not by one's doing something, but by one's *refraining* from doing anything; by remaining still and *being* simply what one really *is*."

To simply "remain aware of the Self" is what "meditation" *truly* means to the Self-realized. It is an effortless, unconstrained perception of ultimate Reality which is the "present awareness," whether one is active or inactive, throughout the waking hours. It is not a matter of attempting to control one's thoughts or restrict one's attention: no matter what is thought, said or done, it is regarded as the doing of the Self, or ultimate Reality. *Whatever* is observed—positive or negative or neutral—"that *too* is It!" This frees one from such (dualistic) concerns as "am I being *aware*? Or was I momentarily focused on some activity and was temporarily *un*aware?"

"When thoughts cross the mind and an effort is made to neutralize them, the effort is usually termed 'meditation'.... Remain as you *are*. *That* is the aim.... To make the mind 'subside'...the mind will remain in an apparent state of subsidence, but will rise again.... What does it matter if the mind is active? It is so only [as] the Self!... Why do you worry 'I didn't' [or 'I did'] meditate?... If the idea 'I did' or 'I didn't' is given up, all actions will end up as meditation.... This, indeed, is the state called sahaja samadhi.... Then 'meditation' cannot be given up. Even if we 'give it up,' it will not let go of us. This is sahaja samadhi [full awakening]."

In the first work he ever wrote (c. 1901, at 22), paradoxically 'practice' amounted to freedom *from* practice. To remain as you are, while realizing *who* you are, is to *practice* being a perfect expression of the Self.

"This is Liberation: never to be heedless of one's own *all perfect* pure Self is the *acme* of...forms of spiritual practice."

Even persons who are acquainted with the historic literature on nonduality (especially English translations) are often familiar with only a few of the terms which are traditionally given in Sanskrit. *Advaita*, which means "not two," would probably be at least one of those known.

An important word, *samadhi*, is one of the least understood. It refers generally to what we might think of as a state of consciousness, and it is characterized in basically three "stages." The first two relate to an effortful or deliberate *intent*, but whose *achievement* remains impermanent.

Savikalpa, the initial phase (also sometimes called *kevala*, which Ramana Maharshi defines as "practitioner") is when the aspirant for Self-realization has grasped the insight that

"Brahman and I are the same actuality." Howerver, in this perspective, there still remains an idea that there *is* an "I" and a "Brahman" which can conceivably coalesce to become a "One"; in other words, there is still a subtle sense of duality in the aspirant's mind.

Nirvikalpa is the state whereby the aspirant's view would have enlarged to, "all is Brahman." But this recognition is temporary, it "comes and goes." For example, this might dominate one's awareness when sitting in meditation, but at varying times later—"back in real life"—the unitive awareness is occluded.

Beyond nirvikalpa is *sahaja*, which means "natural"—in the sense of ordinary (Buddhists would say, "nothing special" about it). Such distinctions even as "all" and "Brahman" are transcended: "Not two, not one," as the Vedas say. Since "there is nothing from the start," there need be no effort to achieve or retain any *particular* state of awareness. Sometimes also termed *sahaja nirvikalpa samadhi* (or simply *sahaja samadhi*), it is the embodiment of Self-realization (or enlightenment) which we would phrase as Absolute awareness.

If you're looking for an equivalent for the word *samadhi*, it is not "trance," it is not "bliss," it is "embodiment" of Self-realization. The word *enlightenment* could be a replacement, too, where Ramana states, "Samadhi alone can reveal the truth."

If you were looking for a subsidiary word, you could apply *clarity*. "The tranquil clarity, which is devoid of mental turmoil, alone is the samadhi which is the firm base for liberation."

And anything conceived as samadhi which is lesser than, or short of, sahaja is not the full extent of samadhi. "Those that are in the kevala nirvikalpa state are not realized, they are still seekers."

The seeker still retains a dualistic bias, however subtle. He will suppose that there is a someone (even himself) who is somehow apart from ultimate Reality: and by doing (or not doing) something, the gap can be closed and "union" result. But: "Remaining in the primal, pure natural state *without effort* is sahaja nirvikalpa samadhi."

An attempt to "close the gap" through "practice" is not what Ramana means by the "natural state." For instance,

> "Meditation is initiated and sustained by a conscious effort of the mind. When such effort entirely subsides, it is called samadhi.... Meditation is a forced mental process, whereas samadhi lies beyond effort.... The *cosmic* mind, being not limited by the ego, has nothing separate from itself."

Sahaja is not about falling into a temporary trance, or experiencing an orgasmic or "oceanic" bliss: rather, it is the dissolution of the subjective "self," and its person-alized identity, into the awareness of the inescapable presence of infinite Be-ing. "When we are always in that state, not going *into* samadhi and coming *out* again, that is the sahaja state. In sahaja, one sees only the Self..."

It is when one is...

> "...*merging* in the one Reality underlying all the phenomena, the Being which is the one reality giving rise to all thoughts, this state is said to be sahaja...You realize that you are moved

by the deeper Self within, and are *unaffected by what you do or say or think*...and that *everything is being done by something* with which you are in conscious union...One who...will not lose his samadhi state...whatever external work he does, and whatever thought may come to him—that is called sahaja..."

Ramana says the naïve idea that samadhi is a dropping into and out of unconsciousness would matter not, even if it were true: *whatever* state or condition of observable existence, it is a manifest expression of the Self, or Being.

> "What does it matter whether body consciousness is lost or retained? *When lost, it is samadhi; when retained, it is samadhi*: that is all. ...If those who have all the Upanishads and vedantic tradition at their disposal have fantastic notions about nirvikalpa, who can blame a westerner for similar notions? ... Samadhi is one's *natural* state. It is the undercurrent in all the three states of waking, dreaming, and sleeping."

Ramana emphasizes that sahaja is the awareness that the seer (I) and the seen (other) are always and only *one*, or Self: the nondual (rather than the dualistic) perspective. Those in that state "cannot find anything which is different from themselves. But to those who do not reach that state, everything appears to be different from themselves.... In the perfect state, there is neither subject nor object: there is nothing [apart] to see...

> "A strong conviction that 'I am the Self' is necessary, *transcending* 'mind' and *all* phenomena.... The artificial 'I' is a projection, and through it one must look to the true Principle.... One has to know what samadhi is. And how can you know it without knowing your Self? If the Self is known, *samadhi* will be known automatically.... To be one's own Self is *samadhi*. The Absolute consciousness is our real nature.... What is samadhi? One's own *true nature*.... In that state, there is

Being, alone. There is no you, nor I, nor it; no present, nor past, nor future. It is beyond time and space, beyond expression [thought]. It is *ever here....*

"Samadhi is holding onto the Reality while witnessing the world, without reacting to it from within—the stillness of a waveless ocean.... Consciousness which is Absolute and unaffected: that is samadhi.... Sages say that the state of equilibrium which is devoid of the ego is samadhi."

Someone posed to Ramana: "It is said in the Mandukya Upanishad that samadhi must necessarily be experienced before attaining liberation."

Ramana replied, "It is stated not only in the Mandukya Upanishad but in all the ancient books. But it is *true* samadhi only if you know your Self."

The Ribhu Gita, which Ramana sometimes quoted, says: "Remaining alertly aware...devoid of differentiation [duality]— even while being engaged in the activities of worldly life—is called the state of sahaja samadhi: the natural state of abidance in the Self."

The jnani Mata Amritanandamayi (better known as Amma):

"By meditating on a form, *savikalpa samadhi* [perception of the Real while retaining the sense of *duality*] can be attained. When one sees the *form* of the beloved Deity, the attitude of 'I' is there, thus there is duality."

"In the state of *nirvikalpa* samadhi there is no entity to say '*I am Brahman*'."

"In 'formless meditation' [sahaja], since there is no trace of 'I-ness', the attitude of duality is completely destroyed."

"What will samadhi be like? *No happiness or sorrow.* There is no 'I' and 'you'. This state can be compared *to deep sleep,* but there is a difference: in samadhi, there is full awareness. Only when we wake up, I, you, and the world emerge. We give reality to them due to our ignorance."

Muruganar, a poet, and awakened disciple of Ramana:

"To remain in the state in which consciousness of the supreme Reality is not lost, even during activities, is sahaja.... Sahaja [is the] state that exists...in such a way that it is not possible to *separate* from it.... Without desirelessness [un-intention], the abiding experience of sahaja samadhi will not ripen.... Until that state of sahaja...there is no liberation for the individual, irrespective of what *other* state one may experience."

A later follower of Ramana, David Godman:

"Sahaja *means* 'natural'...the *direct* experience of the Self, in which no differences or *distinctions* arise. Sahaja nirvikalpa samadhi is the *definitive* state of realization, in which one can live a normal—*natural*—life, fully aware of the Self at all times....

"Experience of Realization is known as samadhi. It is often supposed that samadhi implies trance, but that is not necessarily so. It is also possible to be in a state of samadhi while retaining full possession of human faculties. In fact, a Self-realized sage [such as the Maharshi] is permanently in such a state...

"When one is established in one's true state, one knows the Truth by direct experience. Such a one is 'sahaja nishta', one who is established in the natural state of the Self."

Ramana, in summary:

"The sahaja state: that is realization, for certain.... The *ever-present* state is the *natural* state, sahaja.... The reason for... emphasizing sahaja samadhi [is that] one should be in *spontaneous* samadhi—that is, in one's pristine state—in the midst of every environment.... The Absolute consciousness is our real nature.... Samadhi [is] one's own true nature."

True peacefulness means being okay with whatever condition or effect is present. To be in whatever the present condition is, and to be dissatisfied with that condition is not peaceful.

This may seem obvious, but people often don't follow this obvious pointer to its logical conclusion: when one circumstance is not viewed as more preferable than another, then we are not desiring a particular effect; therefore we are at peace with whatever condition or effect is present—even if the present condition is not one that would be defined as "peaceful".

A true example, from a recognized master (Ramana): He was sitting quietly, after dark, doing nothing—"meditating". He heard someone enter the enclosure where he was. The intruder began looking around, evidently intent on theft. Ramana approached, to tell the man that nothing of value would be found there. The man, seeing him, struck him on the leg with a club. This did not make Ramana "happy": he shouted, "Now hit me on the other leg, if you must!" Startled by the shout, the man fled.

The sage, in meditation, is neither at peace nor not at peace: he is one with whatever condition happens to be present. He is not desirous of one circumstance being present over another.

Thus, even if the mind is agitated—and seemingly not at peace—the awareness of the sage is even "at peace" with that.

Even when Ramana shouted out in anguish, his innate "peaceful state" was not disturbed.

Nor was it to be further disturbed by emotional or mental turmoil resulting from his awareness that he *had* shouted in outrage.

With whatever condition or circumstance that happens to be present—his agitation, or even regret for that agitation—he is uninterruptedly undisturbed in his all-inclusive awareness.

With nondiscriminatory serenity, it matters not where or in what condition one abides. All is the same. Peacefulness is *there*, not somewhere to be sought and subsequently "found".

The key is not in cultivating a meditative mind, but to recognize that a meditative mind (as Krishnamurti would say) is "choiceless".

Bear in mind, there is no universal law which dictates that you must *like* whatever it is that is going on. But there is no universal law that requires that we maintain an emotional attachment to our *dislikes / likes*. We can safely assume that Jesus did not "like" being crucified. But he "didn't take it personally". Ramana probably didn't "like" dying with a painful cancer. But he didn't go around crying, "Why me, why me?!" Who, in their right mind, would like to be in that situation? But Jesus, Ramana and others have attempted to demonstrate by example that it is possible to comprehend that even what we don't like, "that too" is a manifestation of infinite Being that rains on the just and the unjust.

Ramana Maharshi was sometimes asked "Is Self-realization a matter of grace, a gift that is allotted to some worthy few?"

Ramana responded, "It is grace that you are *inquiring*, that you are seeking to merge with ultimate Reality."

"Grace" is not a word often used by non-Christian spiritual teachers. However, it is sometimes used to refer to what might be called the "gift"—really the impetus—of the arising, within one, of the seeking of the sought. As Ramana has put it, "that you are *possessed* of the quest of the Self is a manifestation of the divine grace....The deep inner movement (towards Self-realization) *is* grace....

"Introversion is due to grace; perseverance is grace..."

You now are graced with this inquiry into the nature of universal truth.

When you light a flame to one corner of this page, consummation takes place of its own accord. Allow the spark of your attraction to Self-realization to ignite an all-encompassing flame.

> "For *everyone*, it [awakening] is undoubtedly possible."
> –Ramana

H.W.L. Poonja, who died in 1997, searched India for a teacher of enlightenment. He has said that, until he found Ramana Maharshi, all he ever met were "businessmen in robes."

Finally he met Ramana; he described the experience of an altered state of consciousness which frequently occurred to him, and he asked Ramana if this was enlightened consciousness or Self-realization.

Ramana said, "Is that present now?"

"No, not at the moment," Poonja replied.

"Then that is not what you're looking for," Ramana told him.

One of the most common refrains that an Advaita teacher hears is, "I once had a taste of the experience of Oneness, but it evaporated and I haven't been able to bring it back."

Whatever it is that you expect to experience, if it is not present right now, then that is not the "realized" condition that you're looking for.

This being the case, the Self which you are looking for would have to be the composition of all that you see—and you, as the seer.

So, for the enlightened, Absolute awareness is not a special condition, state or unrepeated "experience". It is one's continual realization that not anything could ever, under any circumstance, be separate from omnipresent Being.

Abandon the expectation that you will encounter the Self at some time or place in the future, or "experience" such an "event" *again*. You do not "approach" That which you already are. Self-realization is merely recognizing that not anything has ever been apart from That which is without limitation in its ubiquitous presence.

Understanding Ramana, Poonja ceased to cultivate psychic abilities.

Ramana said psychic experiences, or even powers, are "mere phenomena...only transient...not worth striving for."

Specifically, he is quoted as saying "there is no wisdom in the one [cultivating] them. [Psychic powers] are not worthy of any thought. Self-realization alone is to be aimed at and gained."

The wisest person takes this view: the foremost priority is Self-realization. *If* psychic experiences then manifest, that would be a by-product. There is a possibility that such an occurrence can happen—but not the other way around.

And where there "is no person," where is the repository of extraordinary "powers"? If Ramana were asked, "Are such powers real," he'd typically respond: "As real as *you* are."

About a dozen times in *Talks With Ramana* alone, he was asked questions such as, Does a self-realized teacher have, or need, siddhis (supernatural powers)? His responses were unequivocal.

> "Such 'powers' manifest only when there is the ego. The Self is beyond the ego, and is realized when the ego is eliminated...The *one* [powers] requires effort to achieve, and the *other* [Self-realization] does not....Where is the use of occult powers for a Self-realized being?...

> "The only permanent thing is Reality; that is, the Self....All the rest is mere phenomena—in It, of It and by It....[Powers] are only transient....All these 'wonders' are *contained* in the one

changeless Self....The force of [one's] Self-realization is far more powerful than the use of all other powers....

"People anxious for siddhis are not content with their idea of Self-realization, and so want siddhis associated with it. They are likely to neglect supreme happiness, to settle for siddhis, [while] a Self-realized person will not waste even a thought on them. Let them get *that*, and then seek siddhis if they so desire! There is no realization in the one who displays them.... Self-realization alone is the aim to be gained....

"Occult powers will not bring happiness to anyone, but will make him all the more miserable....Why aim for that which is not essential, but apt to prove a hindrance to realization?"

Continuing the words of Ramana:

"The jnani [Self-realized] has no doubts [about] himself....He has no doubts, to be cleared....

"So long as false identification persists, doubts will persist... Doubts will cease only when the [individuated identification] is put an end to. That will result in realization of Reality. There will remain no 'other' to doubt."

Full Self-realization leaves no doubt about the actuality of Oneness, of nonduality. And in Self-realization the subject/object polarization is transcended, so that the false identification of the subject self and objective "other" (material, or immaterial such as "special" experiences) no longer engenders separation, or what amounts to the denial of Oneness.

An aspect of the realization of this truth is that one *confronts* the question of "If there is no self, what operates in what is perceived as 'my mind'?"

In the same sense that there is no *material* entity, or form, which is independent of the single, unbroken movement of That, there is likewise nothing *immaterial* that is independent of this same ground of being.

In other words, where it is recognized that there is no such individual configuration as "my" self, it is also recognized that there can be no such configuration as "my mind."

The jnani is aware that there is a concept of "a mind" and there is also, in awareness, a concept that this mind produces "thoughts": but where the conception of the self is absent, the conception of "my mind" is unsupported; and where the conception of the mind is viewed as false, the conception that this mind produces "my thoughts" is also viewed as false.

Who, or what, is this which has conceived the form of the "self"? Whatever is the producer of the sense of self must also be the producer of that sensed self's perceived thoughts; and likewise what we personalize as "my actions," which are a consequence of what is presumed to be "my thoughts."

So, for the jnani there is simply the awareness of the organism and its activities, without personalizing, or identifying with, the assumed process which animates or motivates the organism's activities.

This is finally what is meant by, "You are not the doer."

Ramana: "The mind is only a projection from the Self... one should not even care for the result of the actions.... One remains a witness to them without any attachment.... They are not your own.... Do not think that you are the doer."

Some *transcend* the state of *incomplete* awareness of their always-already existing presence *as* the One, and recognize that *whatever* they do (or *don't* do) is ultimately without significance. This is called *sahaja samadhi* (which literally means "steady state"); effortless, full, and lasting realization of One's true nature. In sahaja, Ramana says,

[You] are unaffected by what you do or say or think.... [It] is the definitive state of realization, in which one can live a normal, natural [unencumbered] life, fully aware of the Self at all times.

As per Ramana: "If the thoughts 'I did' and 'I didn't' are given up...[this] indeed is the state of sahaja samadhi."

Since those who are mired in dualism think in terms of "good" and "bad", they will evaluate acts as "good" or "bad". They will likewise evaluate "consequences" in the same manner.

Therefore, the idea is that "good acts" are followed by "good consequences"; "bad acts" lead to "bad consequences".

This is the (dualistic) idea of (separate) "cause" and "effect": a "good act" (cause) leads to a "good consequence" (effect). Herein is the *idea* upon which "karma" rests.

What Ramana is saying is that *all* "events" or "acts" or "actions" are none other than the Absolute, or Self, in its endless appearances. "Good acts" are Self-expression. "Bad acts" are Self-expression. "Good consequences" are (more of the same) Self-expression. "Bad consequences" are (the same) Self-expression. "Karma" is just an idea, based on the dualistic ("ignorant") assumption that there is something (nameable) *other* than the Absolute, or Self.

An example (Christian): Believe that Jesus rose from the dead (your "action") and your person-ality will survive *your* dead body and be transported to a paradise ("consequence" of your action).

Another example (Hindu): Do puja every day, and your person-ality will survive your dead body and be successively born into a new body, as many times as necessary until every one of your worldly (dream) actions is perfect.

These ideas appeal to those who think in terms of (separate) actions: "birth" event, "death" event, for example.

"Find the root of karma", *dualistic thinking*, "and cut it off"— relinquish the supposition that there is a "this", on the one hand, and a "that", on the other hand (such as "cause/effect", "birth/death", "good/bad", etc.).

Another supposition concerns those who believe that if they're not experiencing giddiness or euphoria, they could not be Self-realized. Their idea is that enlightenment ought to provide at least the thrill of a roller coaster ride, only just more persistently. *Ecstasy* is a product created in an illicit lab, it's not a reward for awakening from self-centeredness.

There is, indeed with Self-realization, a feeling of relief or release, a relaxation of tension, and a sense of peacefulness: because now there is no "self" to fret over, no "others" to chronically react to, nor even a "God" to be petulantly judged by. There is a placid state of contentment for which the word "bliss," misleadingly, comes nearest to describing.

This bliss is more accurately defined as *equilibrium*, a recognition that all things are equal in their sameness of ultimate, or absolute, nature. In the Sanskrit scriptures, the word is *ananda*; and it is clearly a consequence of Self-realization. The constant abiding in ananda is what is known as sahaja samadhi, the perception of "no self."

As Ramana states:

> "There is no difference between the enlightened and the unenlightened in their *conduct*: the difference lies only in their *perception*. The unenlightened identifies himself with the ego... whereas the ego of the enlightened has been lost...
>
> "To realize bliss, one realizes the Self.... Self-realization is bliss; it is realizing the Self as the limitless.... The ego is lost, and bliss remains.... Thus the Self is realized, and bliss results.... Bliss consists in not forgetting your Being."

If an ecstatic state is what you are interpreting as ananda, Ramana adds,

> "...you feel great bliss and happiness and want to stay in that ecstasy. Do not yield to it, but pass on to the next stage which is great calm. The calm is higher than ecstasy and it merges into Samadhi."

In identifying with a self-affirming phenomenal sensation, there remains a subtle duality. But the source of the phenomena and the organism experiencing it are the same one, omnipresent Self. Ecstasy can become,

"...an obstacle, because [in that state] a feeling of *separation* from the *source* of ananda, enabling the enjoyer to say '*I* am enjoying *ananda*', is present. Even this has to be surmounted. The final stage of Samadhi has to be reached in which one *becomes* ananda, or *one with reality*. In this state, the duality of enjoyer and enjoyment ceases in the ocean of sat-chit-ananda, or the Self.... *Be* the Self and *that* is bliss."

Bliss is a word that the jnanis use, but by that term they mean the sense of freedom and *equanimity* that comes with having transcended *attachment* to "states," and the *expectations* that pertain to them. Put another way, bliss is the aspect of Self-realization which leaves one "care free" as a consequence of the *recognition* that "ultimately, nothing really matters."

What is *not* bliss, Ramana says, is "thinking that the world is real"; therefore a concern that some "states" are more significant than others. "[The Self-realized] looks on everything with *unconcern* and remains blissful."

An associated subject is that of love: an entire book could be written on how love is perceived by an enlightened being.

I think we can agree that we are not considering love in its common conception as mere affection and attachment toward another person or object; benevolent concern for other animate beings; romantic or sexual attraction; or worship and devotion toward an idol or supernatural image. All of these are relationships which reflect a dualistic perception. As Ramana Maharshi has said of this, "When you talk of 'love', there is duality, is there not: the person who loves and the entity...who is loved."

In the *transcendence* of the *dualistic* perception is the profound love which the nondual sages refer to. The Sanskrit term *ananda* is often translated into English as "bliss," but the bliss is the consequence of experiencing unconditional love: the word *unconditional* is defined as "absolute." This is love for all that exists: that means the "good," the "bad," and whatever is in between. It means a love that inclusively makes no distinction between what is manifested, from moment to moment, and the omnipresent Totality which manifests it.

Ramana uses various words to indicate the ever-present actuality, such as God or Self; that to which all things owe their be-ing. So he says, "expansion of love and affection would be a [proper] term for a true devotee of God," or the sublime Presence. But he emphasizes that this infinite Presence "is not 'somewhere else', but is inside [as well as outside] of each of us; so, in loving *all*, one loves only the *Self*.... The individual is not separate from God."

He is telling us that *this* love and affection expands to embrace the good, the bad and the indifferent—in *ourselves*, equally as in *others*. This is the "unconditional" aspect, which relates to our being nonjudgmental and non-interfering, and thus eliminates conflict, inward and outward.

This "love" is not an alternative to "hate"; it's the transcendence of divisive polarities: such as that some people, or developments, are "good" or "bad"; or that they *should* be this way, and *should not* be that way. This is what Ramana means by "the *absence* of love *or* hatred."

The infinite Being is above hatred, and above love as well, in the discriminating sense. But that, within each of us, which has the capacity for the expression of unconditional love, or compassion, is a manifestation of the Presence which loves itself through the medium of being all things which can be the subject of love.

Thus Ramana says:

> "Love is not *different* from the Self...[in this sense] God is love.... Love itself is the actual form of God.... Call it pure bliss, God, or what you will.

> "It is only through *jnana* [Self-realization] that the bliss that derives from true love will arise.... Die yourself [into the eternal Self] and lose yourself, becoming *one* with love.... To be the [nondual] Self, that you really are, is the only means to realize the bliss that is ever yours."

So, in summary: God *is* love (as well as all else), and this God manifests as *all* that is.

A natural question which arises when one undergoes a benign shift in consciousness is, "How can the life-changing shift, that I've experienced, be communicated to others?"

First of all, awaken to the life-changing truth that is known as Self-realization; and (second) assist others in discovering that personal change of heart.

But from the standpoint of a person once Self-realized, this question takes on an even deeper significance. And the answer to this question is not likely to be comprehensible to other than the Self-realized person.

There is a fundamentally different view of our world from the standpoint of enlightenment, as contrasted to the perspective of dualism. This is summarized by a comment of Ramana

Maharshi: "So long as identification with the body ['I'] lasts, the world seems to be outside us."

In other words, to the "individual" mind, there is "me" and all else that is "not me"; among the things we conclude are not-me are "the world" (or cosmos).

That the "world" is a concept, or idea, is plain: in deep sleep, both the perception of a me *and* the world are entirely absent. As Ramana puts it,

> "It is only the 'individual' mind that sees the world. When this mind disappears, the world also disappears.... The world appears when you wake up [from sleep]. So where is it? Clearly, the world [awake or dreaming] is in your thought.... The mirror reflects objects; yet they are not real, because they cannot remain apart from the mirror. Similarly, the world is said to be a 'reflection in the mind', as it does not remain in the absence of mind."

Consider: if there were no conscious minds, would there be anything to *say* that there was such an independent construct as a "world"?

So, how does the enlightened perceive what, in dualistic terms, is referred to as the world? From the perspective of nonduality, there is only one, indivisible actuality: the Absolute (or Ramana's term, Self; to others, God). Therefore, there exists no individuated, part-icularized "me," nor conceived "not-me." When we come to realize the truth of this cosmic viewpoint, this is called "Self-realization"; you know who or what "you" are: no thing. When the 'I'—as subject (or seer)—is shown to have no validity, the conception of "separate" objects is also deconstructed.

"Find out what *you* are, and then you understand what the world is," Ramana points out.

> "Duality of subject and objects are your *thought* creations.... Do you not [nightly] create a world in your dream? The waking state [in which you 'see' the 'world'] is also a long, drawn-out dream."

This might be summarized as: the world is as real as a dream; a dream is an illusion. To realize the "true nature" of the "world," one must first realize that the true nature of both you (and all "others") *and* the world is the Absolute (Self).

Ramana: "If we first know the Self, then all other matters will be plain to us....Therefore, one must know the Self, before the world is known."

Here is the nub of what Self-realization tells us: if the true nature of *all* seers is the Absolute, then both those who see the world as "real" and those who don't are equally a manifested activity of (or by) the Absolute. The former is concerned about the existence, or activities, regarding the world; the latter does not recognize the world, or its activities, to be other than the Absolute.

Thus Ramana says:

> "The world is created by the 'I', which in its turn arises from the Self.... The unenlightened takes the world to be real, whereas the enlightened sees it only as a manifestation of the Self. So then it becomes immaterial whether the Self *manifests* itself, or *ceases* to do so [as a 'world'].... The Self is infinite, inclusive of all that you see. There is nothing beyond it, nor apart from it.... The power which has created you has created the world.

If it can take care of you, it can similarly take care of the world, also."

This is what has been said as "*Thy* will, be done."

And, here, we come to the potentiality for peace in the relative world: the nonattachment which allows the 'what is' to *be* what it *is*.

Ramana said to someone who was highly agitated about the affairs of the world, "Can you stop the wars, or reform the world?"

"No."

"Then why worry yourself about what is not possible for you?"

What, then, are we to do?

> "First set yourself right, and *then only* set out to improve 'others'. Change the *hearts* of men, and the *world* will surely change. But one must begin somewhere, and one can begin only with oneself.... When one is not oneself at peace, how can that one spread peace in the world?... When the Self is known, all 'others' become known. Self-realization is, hence, the primary—and sole—duty of mankind."

A connected concern is our conception of pain, largely in our fear of death. The same dualistic perspective is common to both concerns: pain and the "victim" of pain; death and the victim of death. Pain, like death, is viewed in a different context by one to whom such (oppositional) propositions holds no significance.

A questioner asked Ramana, "Is there no 'I am the body' idea for the realized person? If, for instance you were bitten by an insect [such as a scorpion], is there no sensation?"

"There is a sensation [pain]", Ramana replied,

> "and there is also the 'I am the body' idea. The latter is common to both the realized and the unrealized—with this difference.

> "The unrealized thinks 'I am the body only.' The realized person knows that all is the Self [Absolute]: 'all this is Brahman' [the questioner's surrogate for the Absolute]."

"If there be pain", Ramana explained, "let it be. It is also the Self."

"The Self is perfect," he added.

In other words, the "body" that the realized sees himself as, is the Absolute. The body that the unrealized sees himself as, is this finite, ephemeral organism.

From the standpoint of Absolute realization, there is no separate phenomena such as "pain" and "me": both merely come and go within the inseparable completeness of the (perfect) Absolute.

This is not to deny that there is a conscious experience of pain, or to suggest that the sage isn't aware of the physical body. It is to indicate that—unlike the unrealized—he doesn't identify with the pain as something in relationship to "himself" which he then supposes he can conclusively affect. His summary: "Let it be."

It is pointless to raise the question, whose pain is it?; or to propose that "I" can do something about "it". There being no "you", whatever is done about it (Ramana would remind) is That doing what it does.

It should be clear to you that the enlightened do "fall sick". Ramana died of cancer, as did Nisargadatta. Buddha evidently died of food poisoning. But what died? This should also be clear to you. The body died. All of these teachers tell you that what they are is "unborn"; what has not had a beginning point does not have an ending point.

Why would one seek miraculous cures, unless one was identified with the perpetuation of the body? In a "dream" world, there are only "dream" "cures". None of the enlightened above (nor Krishnamurti) sought miraculous cures when they were ill. Every illness, and suffering, is eventually "overcome"—with the passing of time.

Ramana points out that in our deepest, dreamless sleep, there is no "I" that is conscious of any objective thing. This is our daily (or nightly) reminder of our non-relative essence. And we are daily reminded of our relative existence, in our waking/dreaming condition: the "I" is an element of this condition, so that we may functionally realize the "purpose" of the organism, during its period of active presence; "I" am hungry; therefore "I" feed the body; then "I" do what this body is inclined to do, etc.

But, at some point, there is no longer the need for an "I", because the aging of the organism has brought it to an end (or some other development has brought it to a premature end). While the "I" disappears with all that it identifies itself with, the impersonal essence (which presents every night in deep sleep) is not dependent on the images of the "I" for its presence; being non-relative, it is not dependent upon anything outside of itself. This was your essence even in the womb, before there was an image of "I".

This essence, this "condition of being", is not "your" essence; it is the essential condition of all that is, of which you—and all else—partake. As in deep sleep, its "characteristic" can only be said to be that of void: no objective thing. No thing that is "conscious" of some other thing. No "I-sense", because there is not some "entity" to sense any thing—form or formless. This is your condition in comatose sleep. It was your condition in the womb. Ramana, among others, is saying that this *pre*-conscious condition is the same as (through life-long continuation) the *post*-conscious condition. We come from knowing nothing, to knowing nothing.

So, of what value is it to acquire "knowledge" during the seemingly-real dream between pre- and post-consciousness? Yes, we need to know a few concrete facts of life in order to physically function. But of what value is any "speculative" knowledge? Buddha—for just this reason, it is said—refused to answer "speculative" questions, those that go beyond here and now. Silence, he indicated, is the door to your non-relative essence.

Ramana has said, "All know that they must die 'some time or other'; but they do not think deeply of the matter."

It has sometimes been said, rightfully, that spiritual awakening—or dissolving into the Absolute, or Self—is "to die while yet alive."

In *this* death, it is the *idea* of being an individual, a person, that ends or "dies." "What is meant by this sort of death? Annihilation of the ego, though the body is alive."

When the egoic self-centeredness has died, we no longer think of the body-mind as the ultimate identity of who, or what, is truly existing here. As a consequence, fear of the non-existence of the body-mind disappears.

> "In that state, there are no individuals, other than the Eternal Existence. Hence there is no thought of death [of a 'me']....If the ego persists, the person is afraid of death [of the *person*]."

Rather, "Let the person find out his *undying* Self and die" into *that* Self.

The Self, or Absolute, is "that of which there is no *other*."

> "*Be* the Self; there will be no *second* thing to cause you fear.... Abide in the ever-present inmost Self and be free of the fear of death.... The fear of death comes only after the 'I-thought' arises.... So long as there is this, there will be fear.... The 'I-thought' arises and, simultaneously, the fear of death also.... Be rid of the 'I-thought': so long as the 'I' is alive, there is grief. When 'I' ceases to exist, there is no grief... The 'pain' is because of the thought of non-being.... But you are as good as dead even in [deep] sleep. What fear is there then of death?"

The concern for the existence of the physical body and the ego-mind, that the person identifies as "me", dissipates when we realize that these ephemeral forms come and go, as do dew drops in the motionless meadow. This peaceful perspective becomes apparent and accessible when we die to the identification with the "individual" self.

"The ego in each one must die.... Whatever is born is bound to die. Kill the ego: there is no recurring fear of death for what is once dead. The Self remains even after the death of the ego. That is Bliss... If this false identity drops away, ignorance vanishes and Truth is revealed.... The fear of death is of the body.... That which is born must end.... They pertain to the body or the mind. The Self exists before the birth of the body and will remain after the death of this body.... If the form is transcended, one will know that the one Self is eternal.... Die yourself, and lose yourself, becoming one with love.... The ego must die. That is the only way."

Nisargadatta too stressed this seminal teaching, succinctly:

"People are afraid to die, because they do not know what is death. The jnani has died before his death: he saw that there was nothing to be afraid of. The moment you know your real being, you are afraid of nothing. Death gives freedom and power. To be free in the world, you must die to the world."

The Bhagavad Gita says:

"The unreal hath no being; the real never ceaseth to be; the truth about both hath been perceived by the seers of the esence of things."

Throughout our lifetime, we're never more than one breath away from non-existence.

Even though we don't consider it as such, we actually experience this non-existence with as much regularity as the passing of the moon. In fact, if we are deprived of this non-existence for more than a few unbroken occasions, we "lose our mind"—go crazy.

Consider it. Each night, for an unnoticed period of time, you are involuntarily absorbed in deep, dreamless un-consciousness: not at all conscious of any earthly reality—including existence of the *person*. Whatever it is that is present in this condition is totally undifferentiated; it has no relationship to the world, or even the cosmos: all that we usually think of as "reality" has *dis*appeared completely. There is not so much as a "self" which remains to *be* aware of the absolute emptiness.

This likewise is the condition which is said to be present in the deepest sublime state of meditation: the "momentary" death of an identifiable self, along with a "transcendence" of the universe in its entirety.

This pure unembellished presence is closest, perhaps, to our word "awareness" (as preferred to "consciousness," since this implies being conscious *of* some thing—for example, self-conscious—and is generally associated with sentient impressions, in the waking state).

It is this condition of formless presence which is universally the organism's primordial—*pre* "existent" or fundamental —condition.

Upon this natural condition is superimposed our waking and dreaming experience; when waking and dreaming consciousness falls away, this remains as the empty screen upon which the individual's self-image had been projected. While waking and dreaming come and go cyclically, (what is called) pure awareness remains unchanged throughout. As Ramana Maharshi said, "Awareness is your [true] nature: in deep sleep or in waking [or dreaming], *it* is the same."

We mistakenly identify our essence with the impermanent organism, the body; we suppose that the body "has" awareness—and that, in physical death, the awareness falls away from the body. Rather, it is that the body falls away from awareness...as it does in deep sleep. Ramana addressed this:

> "Before considering what happens after death, just consider what happens in your sleep....
>
> "When you sleep, this body and world do not exist for you—and this question did not worry you....Did you ask while asleep...where do 'I go' after death?..
>
> "The body which dies: were you aware of it, did you have it, during sleep?...
>
> "Sleep is temporary death. Death is longer sleep....
>
> "There is no ground for even the thought of ['my'] death."

Consider this. If you were to die in your sleep—where you do not even exist—would you know that you had died?

Ramana makes the further point that any thing which can appear and disappear is impermanent. The world, the entire universe, even self-identity appear each day upon awakening—and disappear again from awareness each night. The only thing which remains unchanged is our fundamental, underlying condition. There is that which does not appear and reappear, and therefore is ever-present.

As Ramana put it: "That which does not exist all the time, but exists at one time and not at another, cannot be real." In other words, only that which does not know "death" is permanent and therefore ultimately real and undeniably existent.

This formless awareness was present before the idea of a "you" even came into form, and will continue in *presence* as the illimitable and non-finite Self.

> "At death, the limited mind dissolves in the unlimited mind."
> – Anasuya Devi

The end of the road, for spiritual teachings, is the absence of every*thing*.

It is difficult for those who are looking at these matters to comprehend the full import of what "oneness" means.

Where there is *only* one thing—which is what "oneness" *means*—there cannot possibly be any distinctions, under any circumstances. Therefore, given that situation, no word, concept or idea has any validity whatsoever: all *that* requires multiplicity.

Consider: when you die, this is exactly the circumstance which likely prevails.

Fortunately, we have the capacity to realize, while we are *alive*, that *ultimately* nothing really matters. Considering that, ultimately *nothing* really matters, how much anguish should we invest in our temporal, impermanent, "relative" fixations in the meantime?

One of the reasons I highly regard Ramana as exemplary is that he lived his life as an instructive answer to that question. If one puts as little energy into relating to this world as he did, would one be unwise?

In my estimation, any teaching which assists one to connect with the reality of the sheer emptiness of their existence—in life or death—is a practical teaching.

When this connection to the impersonal noumenon is made, "you" evaporate, teachers evaporate, teaching evaporates. Not anything can remain, not even that which points to That.

Krishnamurti stated that his imperative—the role of the true spiritual exponent—was "to set man absolutely, unconditionally free." Would a person who is "absolutely, unconditionally free" not be free of an attachment to the teacher, and free ultimately of any bondage to the teachings which connected that person to a teacher?

The object of truly spiritual teachings, surely, is not to create a follower of orthodoxy, whose behavior is predictably mechanical or reactive. Robotic compulsion can in no fashion be equated with freedom. Spiritual freedom would suggest an atmosphere for creative, spontaneous action, rather than attachment to patterns and traditions and a program of "do's" and "don'ts."

In other words, consider that the essence of spiritual teachings is not founded upon an intention to instruct one in how to comport oneself in the future, but rather in the necessity of one's *total attention* in this unending moment that is the *present*. This is what it means to be unconditioned, to be deprogrammed, or—at the very least, to be "programmatically divergent."

You are the teacher; you are your teaching; *and* you are the taught. The ultimate teaching is that, ultimately, there is no teaching.

Therefore, from the standpoint of this understanding, *no* teachings are indispensable: all that any of them can tell you is that, in the comprehension of "oneness," there is no "individual" remaining who needs to be taught.

Ramana Maharshi's death resulted from a cancerous limb (arm). He permitted doctors to treat—but not amputate—his arm. Otherwise, he did not concern himself with treatment nor with the predicable outcome of such a condition.

When he became so weakened that impending death was apparent, he was held in the arms of disciples and comforted. Aside from a smile, it is said that the only sign of his death was the cessation of breathing.

According to the reports, Buddha was enlightened; Ramana was enlightened; Nisargadatta was enlightened. We have no way of knowing with certainty what Buddha may have said (if anything) about reincarnation. We do have, on good authority, what Ramana and Nisargadatta taught about this matter.

Someone said to Nisargadatta, "We have been told about karma and reincarnation..." His response: "Leave it all behind you. Forget it." This is a dualistic concept, he said.

Ultimate reality was not born and never dies, he says; that which is born or re-born is within the relative dream—of impermanence. "There is no such thing," he says of reincarnation. Even its premise of evolving perfection is false: "You are already perfect, here and now." In addition, reincarnation would have to be a process in time: ultimate reality is time-less, transcendent of time.

Ramana, too, asks: Did ultimate reality create such an imperfection that reincarnation is needed to correct it? And: Ultimate reality does not "come" from somewhere; how could it "go" somewhere?

A questioner said: "You [teachers] say that I must be reborn." Ramana replied: "No, I don't say so."

Questioner: "Do you not uphold the theory of rebirth?"

Ramana: "No...remove your confusion that you will be reborn."

As for Buddha, would it not be likely that he would point out that if one had such a desire as reincarnation, it is *desire* which one needs to see to an end.

For your own part, in your deepest sleep, the self or the body are no longer a reality. You are neither alive nor dead, so far as you know. Continuation, or lack of it, is not something you need to concern yourself about. The teachers would tell you that you already exist, as ultimate essence, as anything which you could possibly reincarnate as.

In thorough nondual awareness, such a question does not even persist.

A devotee of Ramana at one time complained (within the master's hearing) that after forty years he was having to relocate to a distant town: "What shall I do, away from Bhagavan?!"

Ramana exclaimed to those nearby, "Here is someone who has been listening to my teachings for *forty years*—and now says he is going to be *away* from Bhagavan!"

Remember Ramana, on his deathbed:

"Leave you?! Where could I *go*!"

Selected Couplets of Ramana Maharshi

All are *forms* of God. Because of our sense of *difference*, we think that we are an "individual" person. There is no mistake greater than this in the world!

One thinks that one is separate from God. Efface the notion that you are different from God.

The real [Source] is not located anywhere. It is all-pervasive.

Don't believe that God has any form. The [Source] is all-pervasive. Don't think that it is limited.

The reality that exists is only One. Then how can there be "another"...which is to be seen? All are seeking the [Source] everywhere, but they don't understand.

Is it possible for everyone to know—beyond all doubt, and by direct and immediate experience—that what he knows is really the natural and primal state? Most certainly. For everyone it is undoubtedly possible.

Become nothing. Only a person who is nobody can abide in the [Absolute].

Contact the author
Robert Wolfe
c/o Karina Library Press
P.O. Box 35
Ojai, California 93024

www.livingnonduality.org
livingnonduality@karinalibrary.com

further reading related to this book:
www.livingnonduality.org/ramana

www.ingramcontent.com/pod-product-compliance
Lightning Source LLC
Chambersburg PA
CBHW052128090426
42741CB00009B/2000